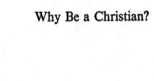

Why Be a Christian?

LAYMAN'S LIBRARY OF CHRISTIAN DOCTRINE

Why Be a Christian?

YANDALL WOODFIN

BROADMAN PRESS
Nashville, Tennessee

4216-46

ISBN: 0-8054-1646-3

Dewey Decimal Classification: 230

Subject Headings: THEOLOGY // CHRISTIANITY

Library of Congress Catalog Card Number: 87-35475

Printed in the United States of America

LIBRARY OF CONGRESS
Library of Congress Cataloging-in-Publication Data

Woodfin, Yandall, 1929-
  Why be a Christian? / Yandall Woodfin.
    p. cm.—(Layman's library of Christian doctrine; 16)
  Includes index.
  ISBN 0-8054-1646-3
  1. Apologetics—20th century. 2. Christian life—Baptist authors.
I. Title. II. Series.
BT1102.W655 1988
239—dc19   87-35475
                                               CIP

To

Berris and Terry Falla,

Joy and Ray French,

Ruth and Harold Pidwell,

Shirley and Brian Smith,

Colleagues and friends at the

       Baptist Theological College in

       Auckland, New Zealand—

Along with May and Arthur Young,

       Our beloved hosts—

Who reflect the beauty of our Lord,

       and their glorious islands.

Acknowledgments

My heartfelt thanks to

the trustees and administration of
Southwestern Baptist Theological Seminary,
especially President Russell H. Dilday,
Vice-President John P. Newport, and
Dean William B. Tolar,

for granting a sabbatic leave and
encouraging me in this project.

Leta, my wife,

whose linguistic ability, love, and
Christian commitment have increased
the joy of this testimony;

Pat Garland and Gloria Wells,

faithful secretaries, whose
work has been graced with patience,
kindness, and encouragement;

Yandall Woodfin

Foreword

The *Layman's Library of Christian Doctrine* in sixteen volumes covers the major doctrines of the Christian faith.

To meet the needs of the lay reader, the *Library* is written in a popular style. Headings are used in each volume to help the reader understand which part of the doctrine is being dealt with. Technical terms, if necessary to the discussion, will be clearly defined.

The need for this series is evident. Christians need to have a theology of their own, not one handed to them by someone else. The *Library* is written to help readers evaluate and form their own beliefs based on the Bible and on clear and persuasive statements of historic Christian positions. The aim of the series is to help laymen hammer out their own personal theology.

The books range in size from 140 pages to 168 pages. Each volume deals with a major part of Christian doctrine. Although some overlap is unavoidable, each volume will stand on its own. A set of the sixteen-volume series will give a person a complete look at the major doctrines of the Christian church.

Each volume is personalized by its author. The author will show the vitality of Christian doctrines and their meaning for everyday life. Strong and fresh illustrations will hold the interest of the reader. At times the personal faith of the authors will be seen in illustrations from their own Christian pilgrimage.

Not all laymen are aware they are theologians. Many may believe they know nothing of theology. However, every person believes something. This series helps the layman to understand what he believes and to be able to be "prepared to make a defense to anyone who calls him to account for the hope that is in him" (1 Pet. 3:15, RSV).

Contents

CONTENTS

1
The Invitation

This book is written because I believe the good news of Christ is true. It is not only relevant, it is essential. It *is* enriching, valuable for our world, and psychologically integrating for persons. But above all it is *true!*

Since this message of hope is true, it is tremendously important for each of us and our times. We live in perhaps the first generation in history to wonder seriously if there will be a future.

And who among us has not felt the chill described in the prophetic parable on the death of God? A madman comes into the marketplace in the morning hours with a burning lantern, announcing that the world has murdered God—the most monstrous deed ever done. Churches are now only the tombs and historical monuments of God. The madman declares:

> We have killed him,—you and I! We are all his murderers! But how have we done it? How were we able to drink up the sea? Who gave us the sponge to wipe away the whole horizon? What did we do when we loosened this earth from its sun? Whither does it now move? Whither do we move? Away from all suns? Do we not dash on unceasingly? Backwards, sideways, forwards, in all directions? Is there still an above and below? Do we not stray, as through infinite nothingness? Does not empty space breathe upon us? Has it not become colder? Does not night come on continually, darker and darker? Shall we not have to light lanterns in the morning?[1]

Many today live as though this dismal prophecy has been fulfilled. The title of a recent book by George Dennis O'Brien reflects this mood: *God and the New Haven Railway and Why Neither One Is Doing Very Well.* [2]

If God is *not* dead, and not dying, but truly lives in Jesus Christ and His Spirit, then the establishment of a secure and joyful personal relationship with Him must be the greatest adventure of life. We can believe with C. S. Lewis that Christianity, "if false, is of no importance, and, if true, of infinite importance. The one thing it cannot be is moderately important."[3]

We Are Embarked

We cannot escape the question of God's existence and His claim upon our lives. He either exists in reality or does not, and we are simply not permitted the luxury of indecision. As Pascal said, we are all already on the journey. We are "embarked." At times we may cherish the illusion that we can refuse to make up our *minds,* but our *lives* in many ways small and large are already being made up.

Seeking to avoid a confrontation with God is like arguing about the existence of air while breathing it, like debating the wetness of water while swimming, or like trying to present a "meaningful" denial that there is meaning in the world. We all, according to the apostle Paul, exist in the very presence of God. In Him "we live and move and have our being" (Acts 17:28). To ignore or escape this living presence is impossible. We need to see the urgency of living in harmony with the divine Being who surrounds us.

One must not only confront the question of *God's* existence but must also decide what to do about *Jesus Christ.* More accurately, one must accept responsibility for the way he or she has *already* decided about Jesus Christ.

Either/Or

Since Christ has in fact appeared in history and claimed to be the Son of His Heavenly Father and the only One who has made God known (Matt. 11:27), each person must now decide not only about God but about Him as made known by this particular person, Jesus of Nazareth. C. S. Lewis focused on this inescapable confrontation with Christ when he reasoned:

A man who was merely a man and said the sort of things Jesus said would not be a great moral teacher. He would either be a lunatic—on a level with the man who says he is a poached egg—or else he would be the Devil of Hell. You must make your choice. Either this man was, and is, the Son of God: or else a madman or something worse. You can shut Him up for a fool, you can spit at Him and kill Him as a demon; or you can fall at His feet and call Him Lord and God. But let us not come with any patronising nonsense about His being a great human teacher. He has not left that open to us. He did not intend to.[4]

We cannot avoid this either/or confrontation. The major purpose of this book is to marshal and illuminate the abundant evidences and reasons for falling at Christ's feet and calling Him Lord and God.

Come and See

Christ Himself is our original model for showing how truth should be allowed to speak for itself. As He called disciples, He welcomed them with a simple yet profound, "Come, and you will see" (John 1:39). He promised that anyone who desired with sincerity and good-will could know assuredly of Him and His truth (John 7:17). When John the Baptist from his prison yearned for more convincing evidence concerning the Christ, Jesus merely answered, "Go back and report to John what you hear and see" (Matt. 11:4). He remained loving and patient with Thomas who refused to believe unless he could see and touch the nail prints in His hands and side (John 20:25).

The same spirit of openness and desire to persuade everyone to believe in Christ moved Paul to write to the Philippians: "I am put here for the defense of the gospel" (Phil. 1:16). The word which Paul used for "defense" is *apologia* from which we get our word *apology* (in the sense of Plato's *Apology* in defense of Socrates after his unjust execution by the Athenians). This is also the basis for our word *apologetics,* the Christian discipline which tries to present the Christian faith persuasively and defensively.

Seeking Common Ground

The Christian believer as a defender or apologist of the faith may on occasion be willing to move onto some common ground also accepted by a nonbeliever. Did not Paul enter into dialogue with the Athenians at Mars' Hill, acknowledge the value of their religious longings, and admit some of the insights of their pagan poets (Acts 17:16-34)? Yet he gave not the slightest hint of compromise or surrender of the Christian message. He almost surely knew the words the poet Aeschylus ascribed to the Greek god Apollo at the founding of the Areopagus upon which Paul stood. That pagan pessimist exclaimed: "Once a man dies and the earth drinks up his blood, there is no resurrection."⁵ Using the very same word which the pagan speaker had used to deny any possibility of resurrection, Paul preached the resurrection of Christ from the dead!

This pattern of dialogue and conviction, which seeks a common ground without compromising the essence of the Christian gospel, is present throughout the New Testament. I pray this spirit will also permeate our evidences and invitation.

The Christian is encouraged to "be prepared to give an answer to everyone who asks you to give the reason for the hope that you have" (1 Pet. 3:15). Believers should never be content merely to parade cold facts or win an argument through sheer logic. We must seek to persuade with gentleness and reverence. Victory in debate is but dust and ashes compared to bringing a person to Christ and Christ's joy. John Newport left a lasting impression on me when, as a seminary student, I heard him explain that our task is "not like David's, to slay Goliath, but to win him to Christ and invite him into the fellowship of the new Israel, the church."

We must admit at the outset that our offering objective evidences and reasons for accepting Christ will not guarantee a personal encounter with God. But the presentation can help break down serious barriers and prepare the way for personal faith. While our task is but a prelude to commitment, it is nevertheless tremendously important. Austin Farrer expressed this conviction well when he wrote, "Though argument does not create conviction, the lack of it destroys belief. What seems to be proved may not be embraced; but what no one shows the ability to defend is quickly abandoned."⁶

While our own witness to the life and ministry of Christ is needed, our Lord Himself teaches that, "No one can come to me unless the Father who sent me draws him" (John 6:44). We give our witness and then wait confidently on the Spirit's creative work to confirm it (Acts 16:14). The human word of witness is but a tool, indispensable but impotent without the Holy Spirit's convincing power and presence (John 16:7-11; Rom. 8:15-16; 1 Thess. 1:5).

The Infinite Risk

How, we may ask, can one be sure that God exists and that He wishes to give His Spirit to convince and illuminate? The answer is simple. No one can know God apart from the risks of faith. A fundamental logic based on the value of life itself may help us here. An early Christian lay apologist, Arnobius, expressed the intuitive wisdom of choosing life. He reasoned that when we are confronted by two alternatives, both seemingly uncertain, "we should believe the one which affords some hopes rather than the one which affords none at all."[7]

This same kind of logic was later used by Blaise Pascal in his famous Wager Argument. He likened the question of believing in God to playing a game of cards where the stakes are infinitely high. If we bet that there is no God and are later proven right, we have only risked a finite life against a finite loss. If, however, we venture that there is no God while in fact there is, we stand to lose the infinite blessings which God's existence would guarantee. Pascal, therefore, reasoned that the odds are *infinitely* in favor of placing our finite lives in the hands of the Almighty God.

To venture is wise, according to Pascal, because the risks of the decisions are unavoidable and the evidences for the Christian faith are clear and compelling. Pascal concluded that the least we can do, when contemplating the alternatives, is to place ourselves in the position of gaining an understanding of God, who is available for faith, and to allow ourselves to be convinced by Him.[8] But don't be foolish and "boast about tomorrow, for you do not know what a day may bring forth" (Prov. 27:1). Christ promised that "whoever believes in him shall not perish but have eternal life" (John 3:16) but warned that those who do not acknowledge Him as Lord in both confession and obedience "will go away to eternal punishment" (Matt. 25:46).

I hope that the evidences and reasons to be presented for the Christian faith will enhance for you the possibilities of a living, personal encounter with the Almighty Father, through the risen Lord Jesus Christ, in the presence and power of the Holy Spirit. These pages are offered in the strong confidence that when we genuinely long to know and experience God, we may, like Pascal, be encouraged by the living Lord who whispers, "Console thyself, thou wouldst not be

seeking Me, if thou hadst not found Me."⁹ At least we may know with
Paul that "God . . . is not far from each one of us" (Acts 17:27).

Christ at the Door

I remember one cold foggy dismal day seeing the great painting by
Holman Hunt, *The Light of the World,* in the Keble College chapel
in Oxford University. A thorn-crowned Christ stands knocking on a
closed door overgrown with vines. The end of the harvest approaches
and fruit lies unclaimed on the ground beneath the trees. The hinges
on the door are rusty and unused. The lantern which Christ holds in
His left hand glows and appears to give off warmth which you could
feel if you cupped your hands around the painted flame.

I gradually became aware that the aged caretaker of the chapel had
put away his cleaning supplies and was standing beside me enjoying
the painting, as he had doubtless done for many years. After a while
he said crisply with the characteristic British gift for poetry, "Even
on the darkest days the light still shines."

This is the heart of the gospel, that "the light shines in the darkness,
and the darkness has not overcome it" (John 1:5, RSV). The light of
Christ's love shines ever brightly. We do not have to despair in the
darkness like the madman with his lantern, grieving that God is dead.
Even now the risen Lord calls, "Here I am! I stand at the door and
knock. If anyone hears my voice and opens the door, I will [come]
in"(Rev. 3:20).

Notes

1. Friedrich Nietzsche, *The Joyful Wisdom,* trans. Thomas Common (New
York: Russell and Russell, 1964), pp. 167-168.

2. George D. O'Brien, *God and the New Haven Railway and Why Neither
One Is Doing Very Well* (Boston: Beacon, 1986).

3. C. S. Lewis, *God in the Dock* (Grand Rapids: Eerdmans, 1970), p. 101.

4. C. S. Lewis, *Mere Christianity* (New York: Macmillan, 1976), p. 56.

5. F. F. Bruce, *The Defense of the Gospel* (Grand Rapids: Eerdmans, 1959),
p. 48.

6. Austin Farrer, "The Christian Apologist," *Light on C. S. Lewis,* ed. Jocelyn Gibb (London: Geoffrey Bless, 1965), p. 26.

7. Arnobius of Sicca, *The Case Against the Pagans,* trans. George E. McCracken, vol. 1, book 2 (Westminster, Md.: Newman, 1949), pp. 116-117.

8. Blaise Pascal, *Pensees,* trans. W. F. Trotter (New York: Dutton, 1947), 233, pp. 65-69.

9. Blaise Pascal, "The Mystery of Jesus" in *Great Shorter Works of Pascal,* trans. Emile Cailliet and John Blankenagel (Philadelphia: Westminster, 1948), p. 135.

2

Being a Christian

Many people who think they do not believe in God are really rejecting a false god, one which does not actually exist but is a product of accumulated fears, imaginations, and misunderstandings. No Christian believes in such an imaginary god either. Similar misconceptions and inadequate beliefs exist regarding Christ and what it means to be a Christian.

Let's Be Specific

Sören Kierkegaard was keenly aware of this problem when he wrote:

> There is something very specific that I have to say, and it weighs so on my conscience that I dare not die without saying it. For the minute I die and leave this world, . . . I will then instantly be infinitely far from here, at another place, where even that very second (what frightful speed!) the question will be put to me: Have you carried out your errand, have you *very specifically* said the specific something you were to say? And if I have not done it what then?[1]

This is also my burden and passion. I want, in the words of the beloved hymn, to "make the message clear and plain." It may be, as Clark Pinnock said, "Misunderstanding the nature of God is the greatest all-time hindrance to becoming a Christian, and understanding Him correctly the greatest incentive."[2]

Faith as *Becoming*

Christ calls us to follow Him. This is an invitation to pilgrimage, to walk through every stage of life by Christ's side, and give Him our total allegiance. Faith in Him involves complete obedience to His values and will for our lives. Few claim to have followed Him perfectly, yet Christ's command for complete surrender is unshakable. Following means more than agreeing with His theology, assenting to truths *about* Him, adopting His code of ethics, or imitating His behavior.

While following Christ does involve these qualities, it means *living* in His presence and power—indeed *being* a Christian. Kierkegaard discerned that it was a sad day in the history of the race and the Christian church when the word *professor* was coined. This word allows for a discrepancy between what we *profess* to be and what we truly *are*. Christ never leaves this option. Believing in Him means being "born again" (John 3:1-3), *becoming* a new person. Paul's language is no less dramatic. He explained, "If any one is in Christ, he is a new creation; the old has gone, the new has come!" (2 Cor. 5:17).

Life at Its Best

This creative transformation and total involvement with Christ received eloquent testimony in the turbulent 1960s when Malcolm Muggeridge, former editor of *Punch,* journalist, satirist, and television personality, announced his conversion. In Muggeridge's opening address as rector of the University of Edinburgh in Saint Giles Cathedral, he affirmed that he had learned that the decision was "Christ or nothing," and he would now endeavor to crown Christ as King. He described the impact of his conversion:

> It means, suddenly to be caught up in the wonder of God's love flooding the universe, made aware of the stupendous creativity which animates all life, of our own participation in it, every color brighter, every meaning clearer, every shape more shapely, every note more musical, every word written and spoken more explicit. Above all, every human face, all human companionship, all human encounter, recognizably a family affair . . . and the majestic hilltops, the gaunt rocks giving their blessed shade, and the rivers faithfully making their way to the sea—all irradiating with this same glory for the eyes of the reborn.[3]

To follow Christ like this means to be open to His creative spontaneity and authority. Those Gadarenes who implored Him to leave their shores (Mark 5:1-19) were unwilling to risk themselves to His dynamic future. This kind of unbelief has always deprived people of the excitement and joy of the Christian life.

Being a Christian means, from the Christmas story until the present day, beholding in childlike wonder the goodness of Christ's coming. G. K. Chesterton described the experience in "The House of Christmas":

> To an open house in the evening
> Home shall men come,
> To an older place than Eden
> And a taller town than Rome;
> To the end of the way of the wandering star,
> To the things that cannot be and that are,
> To the place where God was homeless,
> And all men are at home.[4]

Glory Round About

Long before coming as a baby in a cattle stall, Jesus Christ as Creator-Word is the coauthor and sustainer of all that is good and beautiful. In the fullness of time He was conceived of the virgin Mary. The Word became flesh: He was born in time, space, and history, taking the form of one particular human being. James Stewart of Edinburgh was right when he regretted that two thousand years ago Christ came in the *flesh* and we have been *abstracting* Him ever since! Christ's birth was heralded by the angels with a heavenly glory, but His coming was real and tangible.

When tempted, Jesus rejected the fraudulent offers by Satan of the glories of the kingdoms of this world and trusted solely in the Word of His Father. He began to minister in Cana of Galilee by changing water into wine and "thus revealed his glory, and his disciples put their faith in Him" (John 2:11). He preached beautifully in the Temple, as no one ever had spoken before (John 7:46). With a glory He had before the foundation of the world, He raised Lazarus from the dead (John 11:38-44).

Yet Christ came eventually to the excruciating agony and ugliness of the cross. God transformed the cross by the glory of Jesus' resurrection. When Jesus accomplished that priestly work for our redemption, the veil of the Temple was rent from top to bottom, meaning that we can now go into the presence of the Holy God. The beauty of God's holiness is open to all who are willing to enter and behold. He rose with a glorious spiritual body, ascended to heaven on a cloud, and promised to come again with this same glory.

Reflections from these same scenes and their beauty will shine from time to time throughout our journey with the Lord. Births, weddings, worship, temptations, gravesides, the mysteries of our personal future, and certain death (if He does not return first), are all illuminated by Christ's presence. Our joys are enhanced and our fears calmed as we walk daily with Him.

Biblical language strains to express the wealth and intimacy of the Christian's relationship to Christ. We not only walk with Him but also live "in Him." We live in the memory and glow of His life and teaching. He now surrounds us like the life-giving air we breathe and the radiance of the sun which lights our way. Paul made it clear that when we believe in Christ we are in Him as we live (Rom. 6:11; 8:2) or die (1 Cor. 15:18), speak (Rom. 9:1) or think (Phil. 2:5), toil (Rom. 16:12) or marry (1 Cor. 7:39), greet a Christian friend (Phil. 2:29), remain constant (1 Thess. 3:8), hope and rejoice (Phil. 2:19,24; 3:1).

Following Jesus means walking with Him and sharing His glory. In Westminster Abbey is a tribute to Oliver Goldsmith, one of Britain's leading poets: He "touched nothing that he did not adorn." To Christ this tribute can be made even more truly and profoundly.

We *Need* Him

The only way to begin and live the Christian life is by confessing our need for Jesus Christ. We may continually pray with Helmut Thielicke:

> O Lord, our God, we confess that often we do not like the bodies we have. Sometimes we have longed for the jobs of others. We would like to do away with parts of our history. We are afraid of our moods and feelings. We wish we had more time. We would like to start over again. We lust after the prestige of others. We think more money will solve our problems. We resent the injustices we have suffered and cherish our sorrows. We want to be appreciated for our small graces. We are enchained by the past and enticed by the future. We have never really been understood. In short, we have refused to live because we have held out for better terms. Heal us, O God, from the distance we have tried to put between ourselves and life. Restore to us the love of

thee and all thy creation. Enable us by thy power to be renewed in our whole lives, through Jesus Christ our Lord. Amen.[5]

The one sincere prayer which God *always* answers positively is the one that asks Him to draw near.

I remember seeing an empty hand reaching upward crudely carved in the barren rock in the catacombs of Rome. Those early Christians understood that we all stand before God with nothing to offer but our sins and needs. Everyone must learn to sing: "Nothing in my hand I bring; Simply to thy cross I cling." Jesus underscored this need to confess our absolute dependence on God when He opened the inaugural message for His newly chosen disciples by saying, "Happy are those that know they are beggars in God's eyes" (Matt. 5:3, author's paraphrase).

We come before God not only with empty hands but also with lives in need of His cleansing. According to Mark, Jesus began His ministry by proclaiming, "The time has come. . . . The kingdom of God is near. Repent and believe the good news!" (Mark 1:15). This word *repent* comes from the language of daily conversation and personal relationships. It means to change loyalties, redirect personal goals, turn away from our selfish past, look Christ in the face with love, and be ready to follow Him.

Healing Pain

Any encounter which reveals our lack or need will cause pain. This is especially true when we are convinced of our selfishness and sin. All is not lost, however, for as Martin Luther taught in the realm of the Spirit, "God kills in order to make alive." The task of the Holy Spirit, according to Christ, is to convince or convict us of our sins.

> When He comes, he will convict the world of guilt in regard to sin and righteousness and judgment: in regard to sin, because men do not believe in me; in regard to righteousness, because I am going to the Father, where you can see me no longer; and in regard to judgment, because the prince of this world now stands condemned (John 16:8-11).

This coming of the Spirit to us may be, even as it was for many at Pentecost, a shattering and excruciating experience (Acts 2:1-42). Take heart when this occurs. It is a sign of hope that a wholesome life with Christ is still possible.

When the great Scottish preacher Alexander Whyte was a boy, poverty forced his unwed mother to leave the small child alone in the fields while she worked in the harvest. One season the curious lad ventured too close to a threshing machine and his arm and shoulder were mangled. When the doctor came and probed the damaged areas, the boy screamed with intense pain. But the doctor, to everyone's surprise, said gently, "I like the pain." This meant that enough live tissue and nerve remained for possible healing.

Decades later when Alexander Whyte preached in his church in Edinburgh on the convicting power of the Holy Spirit, he would raise his scarred but healthy arm and say, "I have liked the pain!" When the Holy Spirit comes in searing, convicting power, He will probe the sensitive areas of our moral life and cause pain. This means enough life and conscience remains for the Holy Spirit to heal. We are still capable of repentance and belief in Christ.

Salvation, a Gift

As we repent, we should understand that we do not do this in our own strength. From the beginning of the experience, "God's kindness leads you toward repentance" (Rom. 2:4). George Whitefield perceived this truth and preached, "Let no one boast of how well he repents, for even our repentance needs to be repented of, and our very tears washed in the blood of Christ."

Being a Christian is, from beginning to end, essentially our repentant belief and our believing repentance as we respond to the abundant grace God offers through His Son. Jesus is "the author and perfecter of our faith" (Heb. 12:2). God, the Giver of our faith shows Himself in all of His dealings with us through Christ to be *worthy* of our repentance and faith. Our faith then is simply the appropriate response of taking God at His Word. As Emil Brunner said, "Faith *is* obedience—nothing else—literally nothing else at all."[6]

When we finally realize that our salvation is a gift of grace from God, we feel profoundly liberated. We are all, as James Stewart explained, prone to ask how we can achieve salvation,

> just as Saul of Tarsus asked it in the lecture room of Gamaliel, as Luther asked it in a monastery at Erfurt, as John Wesley asked it in the Holy Club at Oxford. Laboriously these men hewed our their

broken cisterns, toiling to store up their good works and creditable
achievements, their charities, austerities and penances. But for Saul and
Luther and Wesley the day came when their question "How shall I win
salvation?" was answered from the throne of God. And the answer was,
"You can't! Take it at the cross for nothing, or not at all."[7]

Once this gift is accepted, the true and lasting joy of being a Christian
may begin. And the thrilling truth is that the Christian life not only
begins but also continues in grace. We do accept duties and disciplines
along the way, but our obedient responses spring from gratitude for
the grace we have been given and continue to receive.

Surprised by Grace

The realization that salvation is of grace is also tremendously important for the way we seek to present the case for Christianity. While
evidences and reasons for being a Christian will be presented, we must
remember that if the gospel and Christian experience do, indeed, issue
from grace, no *reason* exists for God's being gracious to us. His
election of Israel, His sending His Son, and His invitation to us are
surprising gifts which we cannot explain.

The biblical writers struggled to convey this mysterious quality of
grace when they expressed the belief that Christ knew and chose us
"before the creation of the world" (Eph. 1:4). This means Christ's
coming and offering love are neither historical accident, a result of the
evolution of the race, nor reward for our worthiness, but the products
of God's loving heart.

We may think we can trace the causes and times of our experiences
of grace. We may remember caring parents, devoted pastors, and
Sunday School teachers who shared their faith. I used to think my
Christian life began when as a small boy I began to listen more
carefully to the preaching of Dr. Baker James Cauthen in a summer
revival. One morning I went into the room where my mother was
sewing. I was concerned with my failure to be in every way the person
I wanted to be. I asked her, cautiously, what was the last thing she
wanted to do before she died. She carefully gave me room to breathe
and said, "I'm not sure how I would express it, but what are you
feeling?" I said, "I would want to ask Jesus to forgive my sins." It was
a timid, self-centered stumbling into the Savior's arms. Then and

there I became a Christian. Often I have looked back on that fragile beginning of my faith, but I have also grown increasingly confident of its depth, for still I want my last breath to be in confession and thanksgiving—a childlike prayer.

Sustained by Grace

The stream of grace, however, stretches much farther: to those who witnessed to our primary contacts with the gospel; to early missionaries in our land; back through the ages, sometimes very dark, in church history; and even further, to the New Testament itself. From there the echoes ring through prophets, poets, and patriarchs of Old Testament revelation. Eventually we must come to the untrackable mystery of grace in the very being of God and exclaim with Paul in his doxology:

> Oh, the depth of the riches of the
>   wisdom and knowledge of God!
> How unsearchable his judgments,
>   and his paths beyond tracing out!
> "Who has known the mind of the Lord?
>   Or who has been his counselor?"
> "Who has ever given to God,
>   that God should repay him?"
> For from him and through him and
>   to him are all things.
> To him be the glory forever!
>   Amen (Rom. 11:33-36).

We present our evidences and reasons for being a Christian in this stream of grace. Witnessing will, therefore, be more like introducing a friend and exploring the mystery of his or her love for us than like reporting clinical evidence, engaging in mathematical reasoning, or pleading a legal case.

Faith in a Person

The coming of God in Christ confronts each age, culture, and individual with its own particular stumbling block. To the Jews, Christ's death on the cross was a scandal because it clothed Him in an aura of moral shame and made God appear weak and impotent in the face of suffering and death. To the Greeks, the entrance of God into finite human flesh seemed to compromise the infinity and spirituality of God. To think that one could be saved by looking to the grace of God rather than working it out morally and rationally for oneself was also to them utter foolishness. To the medieval mind the hope that a holy and righteous God would be willing to forgive sin was difficult to comprehend. To our own age, the claim that God is *personal* may be the greatest obstacle to faith.

God revealed the personal dynamic character of the divine name when He declared to Moses, "I am who I am" (Ex. 3:14). This means that God is the eternal One who says, "I." He will be what He chooses to be and will remain into His future to be there for us if we are willing to venture and meet Him personally. A person is, according to Jürgen Moltmann, "an open question addressed to the future of God."[8] A Christian is one who follows God into *Christ's* future.

Being a Christian means trusting our lives to Christ and the values He enshrines. Jesus allowed some of the titles used to describe Him— Messiah, Son of God, Son of David, and Son of man—to be used very dynamically. He did not want these terms simply to be predefined, waiting for intellectual assent. He wanted to allow the encounter with Him to define the concepts within the living relationship.[9] Often He invites us to believe and promises, "You do not realize now what I am doing, but later you will understand" (John 13:7).

Willing to Venture

From the shore Jesus called to His disciples in their fishing boat, "Have you caught anything?" When the answer came back across the shallows that they had not, He commanded them to launch out into the deep. They could have responded in a calculating spirit: "You must be a stranger here and not know much about fishing because we don't catch fish out in the deep, but here along the shore." Nevertheless, they obeyed His command and could not contain in their nets the tremendous catch (Luke 5: 4-11).

Jesus still calls us to venture above and beyond our narrow assessment of life's possibilities. Belief in Him means venture. The ultimate question is not how we *define* faith or calculate our human resources, but how much are we willing to *risk* for Him?

When the authorities of the established church in England threatened John Bunyan with prison to prevent his preaching, he struggled long and hard with his decision. God seemed to be asking him to pull the roof and walls of his home down upon his wife and family, especially little, blind Mary whom he loved with a special tenderness. Finally, determined to preach, he found the heart to write in his diary: "If God does not come in, I will leap off the ladder blindfolded into eternity. Sink or swim, come heaven, come hell. Lord Jesus, catch me if you will, nevertheless, I will venture for your name!"[10] This willingness to venture, not into some vague misty dream or nebulous principle, but in *Christ's name* is specifically, *quite* specifically, Christian faith.

What Does It Cost?

While Jesus grants many blessings to those who accompany Him, He warns followers to count the cost like one who is building a tower or preparing for war. The New Testament is full of stories of those whose illusions were shattered because they followed Him for the wrong reasons: personal gain, a good meal, the shallow excitement of wonders, or the fulfillment of nationalistic hopes. Jesus' path will eventually lead, however, to the loneliness occasioned by His exalted standards of holiness. Sooner or later, most of us will know rejection and possibly persecution by the world as we take our cross and follow Him.

In fact, the first great theological confession of Christ's deity and messiahship—when Simon Peter at Caesarea Philippi acknowledged Jesus as the Christ, the Son of the living God (Mark 8:27 to 9:1) — soon proved to be pathetically incomplete. Simon still lacked the commitment to discipleship which could accept and become personally involved with the cross. Perhaps a greater confession of our Lord was given in full view of the crucified one by the unnamed soldier who declared in awe, "Surely this man was the Son of God!" (Mark 15:39). However that may be, to believe in Christ and follow Him means to be willing to share His suffering love, even if it involves a faithfulness unto death.

The New Testament cautions that only one kind of faith, the faith that *endures,* is adequate for salvation. Although Jesus was speaking about those whose faith would enable them to endure the calamities of God's judgment in the last days, He was also establishing a valid spiritual principle for all ages when He affirmed: "He who stands firm to the end will be saved" (Mark 13:13).

From the earliest days of the church, when Stephen and many of the apostles were martyred for their faith, down to our own time, believers have been willing to lay down their lives for the gospel. Our hearts still quicken at the words of aged Polycarp when he replied to those offering him the chance to escape death if he would renounce Christ: "Eighty and six years have I served Him and He has done me no wrong, and can I revile my king that saved me?"[11]

Whether the Christian is ever called upon to make this sacrifice, the call to discipleship demands a level of commitment which includes willingness to deny ourselves and take up our cross and follow Christ (Mark 8:34). This is no marginal word from Him but is at the heart and center of what it means to *be* a Christian.

Jesus accented this challenge when He warned the disciples to weigh carefully their profession of faith. They confidently told Him: "Now you are speaking clearly and without figures of speech. Now we can see that you know all things, and that you do not even need to have anyone ask you questions. This makes us believe that you came from God." He replied, "You believe at last!" But immediately He cautioned them: "A time is coming, and has come, when you will be scattered, each to his own home. You will leave me all alone." We can be thankful Jesus did not leave His followers with this grim prediction. His parting word is one of assurance and strength: "Yet I am not alone, for my Father is with me. I have told you these things so that in me you may have peace. In this world you will have trouble. But take heart! I have overcome the world" (John 16:29-33).

The Wind Beneath Our Wings

Being a Christian, then, means following Jesus of Nazareth, who never offered a challenge He had not Himself accepted and overcome. He spoke and acted with an authority both compelling and winsome, neither arrogant nor unsure. He asked that we surrender only what is harmful for us and promised in return an enriching spiritual relationship to help us live life at its very best. His challenges and commands are not so much burdens to carry as they are the winds of the Spirit beneath our wings, whereby we may soar beyond our own limits and strengths. The world yearns for these heights through human love, but Christians have found them in Christ's love. The prophet expressed the same longing but claimed God's *promise* when he declared: "Those who hope in the Lord will renew their strength. They will soar on wings like eagles; they will run and not grow weary; they will walk and not be faint" (Isa. 40:31). The Christian can therefore pray with Augustine, "Give what Thou commandest and command what Thou wilt."[12] We may stand alongside those who experienced the early wonders of Christ's resurrection and "still did not believe it because of joy and amazement" (Luke 24:41). It seemed for their staggering emotions too good to be true—but it was, and it *is* true!

Notes

1. *Sören Kierkegaard's Journals and Papers, Auto-biographical,* part II, 1848-1855, ed. and trans. H. V. and E. H. Hong (Bloomington: Indiana University Press, 1978), 6: 476.

2. Clark Pinnock, *Reason Enough* (Downers Grove, Ill.: InterVarsity, 1980), p. 118.

3. Malcolm Muggeridge, Rectorial Address, University of Edinburgh, Scotland, February 16, 1967.

4. G. K. Chesterton, "The House of Christmas," *Poems* (London: Burns and Oates, 1915), p. 59.

5. Helmut Thielicke, Chapel Address at Perkins School of Theology, Southern Methodist University, Dallas, Texas, October 27, 1963.

6. Emil Brunner, *The Mediator* (Philadelphia: Westminster, 1947), p. 592.

7. James S. Stewart, *Heralds of God* (London: Hodder & Stoughton, 1946), p. 85.

8. Jürgen Moltmann, *Theology of Hope* (New York: Harper & Row, 1965), p. 91.

9. Eduard Schweizer, *Jesus* (Richmond: John Knox, 1971), p. 22.

10. John Bunyan, *Grace Abounding* (Chicago: Alex R. Allenson, 1955), pp. 145-146.

11. Roland Bainton, *The Church of Our Fathers* (London: SCM, 1947), p. 15.

12. *The Confessions of St. Augustine,* trans. J. C. Pilkington (Cleveland: Fine Editions, n.d.), book X, ch. xxix, p. 192.

3

Homemade Gods

Religion, according to A. N. Whitehead, is what we do with our solitude, at least what we do with our freedom.[1] How do you spend your free time? Let's explore the ways we invest ourselves in popular culture, and the religious implications will soon become apparent.

People build *civilizations* in an effort to assure their survival. They create *culture* in order to express and possibly enrich their *values.* Culture may enhance the quality of life in a civilization as skills, forms of communication, and arts are developed. At the same time, any cultural expression, whether high or popular, may become an idol. In the higher classical art forms, such as Michelangelo's sculpture, Gothic architecture, or Mozart's music, we may be tempted to enshrine and worship intellectual complexity or aesthetic excellence. In the lower popular art forms, such as soap operas, Western movies, detective stories, country and rock music, and professional sports, we may reverence the easy solutions to problems, the sensual threshold, and the immediacy of our pleasures.

The God Makers

The shape and style of idols may change, but the warning of Isaiah is still relevant. He spoke of a foolish man who cuts down a tree. With some of the wood he made a fire, warmed himself, and cooked a meal. "From the rest he makes a god, his idol; he bows down to it and worships" (Isa. 44:14-17). We are none of us very far from this worship of ourselves and our creations, which is idolatry.

The idolatrous character of much popular culture is confronted with both compassion and courage by John Wiley Nelson in his exciting book, *Your God Is Alive and Well and Appearing in Popular Culture.* He maintained that in America the success of any unit of popular culture is directly proportionate to its ability to perform satisfactorily the religious function of affirming and supporting beliefs already held in the dominant American cultural belief system.

Popular culture is to what most Americans believe as worship services are to what the members of institutional religions believe.[2]

Nelson pursued this thesis, declaring that "every time we watch TV, read popular magazines or detective fiction, listen to country music, go to the movies or professional sports events, . . . we are in fact attending worship services of the American cultural religion fifteen to twenty hours a week."[3]

Cheap Grace

When the whole gamut of human experience is involved, many different kinds of "evil" are supposed to be overcome by popular culture: bad breath, broken romance, national disintegration, racial annihilation, attacks from outer space, collapse of the natural order, failure of nerve, ill health, loss of significant persons, our own death, and many, many others. Proposed solutions to these problems will obviously be many and varied. However, "salvation" comes through a recognizable pattern.

"Salvation" usually involves most of the following characteristics: (1) *oversimplification* of the problem; (2) assessment of the problem as being *external* to us in a way for which we are not responsible; (3) a solution dependent upon some *heroic* individual's resources; (4) some kind of *sacrifice* or loss by the redeeming individual; (5) the granting of an *assurance* that the problem may ultimately be overcome; and (6) frequently the use of some kind of *unethical* means to accomplish deliverance, such as force or deception.

In offering "salvation" from so many evils, popular culture frequently breaks into those supernatural dimensions which are traditionally the domain of religion. The "resurrection" of characters on television shows; books, movies, and television shows that deal with creatures from space; and increased interest in what happens after death are but a few examples of the way popular culture addresses our need for the supernatural. We can identify with some of these longings for the transcendent, but surely we must deplore the shallow grounds we are given for such hopes.

The Forked Tongue

We must be very careful to distinguish between the stated and hidden messages of the medium. A crime story, whether in movie, television, or novel, may give the appearance of being against crime, murder, and violence. Yet the story may contain little respect for human dignity and personality. So much dishonesty, deception, and gratuitous violence may be used in solving the crime that the expressed morality of the story is compromised, and lower values dominate. This kind of double-talk can be easily recognized in television soap operas. The stories appear to be built around the values of home, business, health, and personal fulfillment. Yet the persons which threaten these stated values are often so glamorously portrayed that the higher priorities are completely lost.

A subtle and dangerous duplicity is often present in media portrayals of war. The avowed theme of almost every contemporary dramatic presentation on war is its evil and horror. However, the glorification of heroic but needless sacrifices and unexamined national values may be quite unworthy. Our vicarious enjoyment of the images of aggression and revenge may actually foster emotions and hostilities which lie at the root of wars. Do we not at times come away with the demonic impression that war is inevitable, or at least that it possesses some inherent value? We may even ask if avowed antiwar films do not capitalize on our feelings of national guilt and seek to confirm the now majority opinion concerning our withdrawal from Vietnam? Where were these movies and their supposed morality during the heat of battle?

Be that as it may, Kyle Haselden challenges our sensitivity profoundly when he ventures:

> Every television program, every movie, every bit of literature that exalts modern war and dulls our awareness of its horrors is the most deadly kind of obscenity. Sexual obscenity, even the worst kind of pornography, is a mere nuisance compared with the glamourizing of war.[4]

We should ask if we do not bow down and worship all too frequently, even if unconsciously, at the altar which popular culture has built to Mars, the god of war.

Death in the Fast Lane

There is a parable about the god of progress who went to the head of an African state and promised to build an elaborate system of superhighways for his country and supply the nation with an abundance of powerful and attractive automobiles. The god made these promises on one condition: that the ruler of the nation sacrifice each year 23,000 lives on the altar of progress. When the ruler refused, the god responded, "I do not understand. Every year the United States is willing to offer more than twice this demand."

We may be tempted to think that this parable and the accompanying gruesome statistics merely describe a sociological condition. But do we not in reality worship the gods of speed, power, and convenience? I have no desire to retreat from progress, nor to overlook the sensitive fact that many accidents and deaths occur where those involved are not directly responsible. But again, we must ask about the religious implications of this awesome tragedy in our culture. Why risk and endanger so many persons? The question would have infinite proportions were only one life lost because of our allegiance to these lesser gods.

Olympic Gods

God is surely pleased with physical fitness and the celebration of life and good health by participation in wholesome athletics. The potential for recreation to become *re-creation* exists when athletes demonstrate the mastery of their skills. While I personally do not find in the New Testament any encouragement for Christians to be involved in competition, competitive sports may have some psychological and disciplinary value if our desire to win does not threaten higher personal and spiritual values. At this very point, our generation's near obsession with sports may need a prophetic warning.

We may be grateful for every Christian who is involved in athletics, both amateur and professional, if they seek to influence their associates toward Christian priorities. This appreciation, however, should never hide the many indications that sport, particularly in its professional organizations, is today a major world religion.

Professional leagues have increasingly encroached upon the time, energy, and loyalties which by divine right belong to Sunday, the

Lord's Day. Their association with gambling totals in the billions of dollars each week. They are sponsored by some advertisers whose products are proven to be harmful and unsafe. That is wrong.

The Price of Glory

Let us, however, focus on one simple replay and challenge those sports like boxing, ice hockey, and professional football which are physically most dangerous. Granting that the following excerpt from Augustine's *Confessions* deals with the murderous cruelty of a bygone age, there is still a warning here which we should heed, lest we also become insensitive to the pain of any one of God's creatures caused by unnecessary violence. The setting and narrative sequence need no commentary and the passage is so moving and relevant that it deserves to be read in full. Augustine told the story of his friend, Alypius, who had gone on ahead of him to Rome to study law,

and there he was carried off in an unbelievable way by the unbelievable passion for gladiatorial shows. Although he would have opposed such shows and detested them, certain of his friends and fellow students whom he chanced to meet as they were returning from dinner, in spite of the fact that he strongly objected and resisted them, dragged him with friendly force into the amphitheater on a day for these cruel and deadly games. All the while he was saying: "Even if you drag my body into this place, can you fasten my mind and my eyes on such shows? I will be absent, though present, and thus I will overcome both you and me."

When they heard this, they nevertheless brought him in with them, perhaps wanting to find out if he would be able to carry it off. When they had entered and taken whatever places they could, the whole scene was ablaze with the most savage passions. He closed his eyes and forbade his mind to have any part in such evil sights. Would that he had been able to close his ears as well! For when one man fell in the combat, a mighty roar went up from the entire crowd and struck him with such force that he was overcome by curiosity. As though he were well prepared to despise the sight and to overcome it, whatever it might be, he opened his eyes and was wounded more deeply in his soul than the man whom he desired to look at was in his body. He fell more miserably than did the gladiator at whose fall the shout was raised. The shout entered into him through his ears and opened up his eyes. The result was that there was wounded and struck down a spirit that was still bold rather than strong, and that was all the weaker because it presumed upon itself whereas it should have relied upon you [God].

As he saw the blood, he drank in savageness at the same time. He did not turn away, but fixed his sight on it, and drank in madness without knowing it. He took delight in that evil struggle, and he became drunk on blood and pleasure. He was no longer the man who entered there, but only one of the crowd that he had joined, and a true comrade of those who brought him there. What more shall I say? He looked, he shouted, he took fire, he bore away with himself a madness that should arouse him to return, not only with those who had drawn him there, but even before them, and dragging along others as well.[5]

We cannot dismiss this confession lightly, as though it has no relevance for our contemporary athletic scene. Let us ask ourselves if we have ever been tempted—and some of us have yielded—to being secretly glad during a hard-fought competition when a star performer on an opposing team was injured, thus increasing the possibilities of victory for our side?

The Need for Responsibility

Do not we as spectators share some responsibility for our involvement in any sport which takes such heavy tribute as an occasional death due to injury and causes many debilitating conditions and some lifelong pain? As I write these lines, it is just past mid-season in the professional football year. The National Football League, according to a network newscast, has officially announced 944 injuries so far, with 1,400 expected before the season ends. And in February 1987 the Daytona International Speedway received its seventeenth human sacrifice as driver Joe Young's car was broadsided by another driver coming out of turn three midway through the race.

The Hucksters

Much modern advertising deals with ultimate values and usurps the role of religion. By its continual appeal to our lower motives, it serves as the high-pressure evangelist for the gospel of materialism. It prostitutes the rightful use of language by overloading it with supernatural claims for assorted products. I do not intend to disparage all advertising. Some is in good taste and contributes to our lives by informing us of worthwhile products. However, strong confrontation is needed when the values of truth, personality, and God's creation are deliberately misrepresented and arrogantly ignored.

The Shameless

Some devisers of campaigns apparently feel no shame in declaring to millions that their products add zest to life. The cheap ethics of unfair comparisons and misused generalized statistics are accepted by the trade. In mimicry of the Word of God which has a legitimate function to convict us of our sin, advertising assumes the role of a disturbing spirit to create in us a restlessness and need for its products.

Possibly the greatest misrepresentations in this field come through what is implied or assumed through association. The displaying of merchandise accompanied by beautiful scenes of nature or attractive, famous, or successful people can only distort the truth. Beauty in nature and personal vitality, like all good gifts, come from the Father above (Jas. 1:17). The success or fame of persons is due far more to their gifts, their heritage, determination, discipline, or good fortune than to the use of an erstwhile product.

The Faceless

The religious scope of advertising is probably seen most clearly in its high-pressured dissolving of personal worth. John N. Phelan believes that this tendency to lose sight of the individual is the most threatening problem confronting those who are continually bombarded by the commercial messages of the mass media.

> In tennis, in conversation, in lovemaking, we respond at the level we are addressed. If individuals are really not even being seen, if personal differences are invisible to media managers since they must deal with composite figures constructed by market research, if we then spend large fragments of our lives listening to their message, we risk becoming what they wish we were—facilely manipulated and predictable units, atoms of purchasing power, with all of our needs created by advertising. . . . If media messages, as we have seen, promote the notion that life is a series of problems to be solved by products, audience and readership surveys enhance that view by presenting people as the sum of their certificates and warranties.[6]

But as Christians we can know that our personal worth is not

determined by market research, statistical patterns, or our own idolatrous creations of popular culture, but by Christ's love and personal
will for each one of us. We are, as Paul wrote to the Romans, not to
let the world around us squeeze us into its mold. This means we are
not to be "schematized" according to the schemes or fashion of the
age. Through Christ we can renew even the *categories* by which we
think and evaluate our world, according to the will of God (Rom.
12:2).

Notes

1. Alfred North Whitehead, *Religion in the Making* (New York: Macmillan, 1927), p. 16.

2. John Wiley Nelson, *Your God is Alive and Well and Appearing in Popular
Culture* (Philadelphia: Westminister, 1976), p. 16.

3. Ibid., p. 17.

4. Kyle Haselden, *Morality and the Mass Media* (Nashville: Broadman,
1968), p. 118.

5. *"Augustine,"* *Christian Classics,* "The Confessions," bk. 6, ch. 8 ed.
Douglas L. Anderson (Nashville: Broadman, 1979), pp. 124-125.

6. John M. Phelan, *Media World* (New York: Seabury, 1977), pp. 123-124.

4

To Whom Shall We Go?

When enemies were becoming increasingly hostile and many followers were leaving as His demands became clearer, Christ turned to the disciples and asked, "You do not want to leave, too, do you?" Peter responded with the simple question, "Lord, to whom shall we go?" (John 6:67-68).

Apart from Christ, what other possibilities does one have? What are their strengths and weaknesses? Let us consider a few of the more relevant secular and religious competitors to the Christian faith. These selected models may never confront us in the structured manner of this presentation. I do believe, however, that these contending value systems with their corresponding life-styles are the most formidable alternatives to Christian belief. In the next chapter we will explore some world religions, but first, some secular contenders.

If It Feels Good, Do It

The pleasure philosophy, (called hedonism from the Greek word for *pleasure*) is the most subtle and powerful alternative to Christianity today. Representatives of this life-style range from those in Isaiah's time who said, "Let us eat and drink, for tomorrow we die!" (Isa. 22:13), through Democritus, Epicurus, on down to current carnal philosophies.

In this long history, the priorities of pleasure have been defined and emphasized in many ways. The common element seems to be the feeling that immediate experiences of pleasure, whether experienced through the mind (contemplatively) or through the body (sensuously), are worthwhile in and of themselves. The pleasures are valuable for themselves and are not to be evaluated by their consequences.

Three basic tenets are held by most hedonists:

(1) Pleasure is good and desirable as a *goal* to be experienced.

(2) *Only* pleasure is good and nothing other than pleasure is ever desirable as an end.

(3) The greater *quantity* of pleasure has more value than, and is always desired in preference to, the lesser.[1]

The view that pleasure can be derived from doing good things for others is not hedonism. This view builds on a belief—possibly unacknowledged—that *reality* is interested in and capable of sustaining one's intention until it creates some benefit for another person. Furthermore, to derive pleasure from doing something for others which will not produce good results until some later time (like planting trees under which we will never sit) demands a view of time and space which an *immediate* experience of pleasure alone can never provide.

Body *and* Soul

Hedonism falsely promises to relieve us from the responsibility of acting with integrity toward the *unity* of ourselves as soul and body. It seeks to drive an unnatural wedge between the spiritual and physical parts of our human nature. On the one hand, we may be tempted to retreat into a psychological state of well-being, ascetically denying the instinctual drives and desires of our physical bodies. On the other hand, we may try to avoid spiritual responsibilities by allowing ourselves to be dominated by sensual pleasures.

But *Which* Pleasures?

Hedonism fails to deal adequately with pleasure or happiness because of its own inner contradictions. It may lean toward a physicalism that evaluates pleasures in terms of biological, quantitative intensity which lead to physical exhaustion. Then the hedonists must realize the limits of their perspective and cry out for *wisdom* to discern between the values and effects of different *kinds* of pleasures.

In the ancient world many Epicureans, who claimed to live solely for the pleasures of eating and drinking, did not fully understand their master's philosophy. Epicurus taught:

> When, therefore, we maintain that pleasure is the end, we do not mean the pleasures of profligates and those that consist in sensuality, as is supposed by some who are either ignorant or disagree with us or do

not understand, but freedom from pain in the body and from trouble in the mind. For it is not continuous drinking and revelings, nor the satisfaction of lust, nor the enjoyment of fish and other luxuries of the wealthy table, which produce a pleasant life, but sober reasoning, searching out the motives for all choice and avoidance and banishing mere opinions, to which are due the greatest disturbance of the spirit.

Of all this the beginning and the greatest good is prudence. Wherefore prudence is a more precious thing even than philosophy.[2]

Happiness as By-Product

When we live for pleasure or happiness alone we never find them. Happiness comes only as a by-product of our accepting higher values. Aristotle expressed this principle long ago: "Happiness will never be found if directly pursued." He called it "the hedonistic paradox."[3] Thus, seeking pleasure or happiness for one's self is like a foolish person walking along a railroad track expecting that somewhere the rails will meet. They never do.

We need to accept ourselves as soul and body. The body is that piece of the world which we ourselves *are.* Since the body is a gift from our Creator, we are *responsible* for it. As souls, or persons, we must choose wisely how we use our bodies. At times we need to forego certain pleasures in order to live worthily toward God and others. We should seek, then, to live an abundant though disciplined life. Let us claim an ancient promise which can now be clearer and surer through Christ: "The Lord bestows favor and honor; no good thing does he withhold from those whose walk is blameless" (Ps. 84:11).

Nothingness, with a Hole in It

Another alternative to Christian belief is nihilism, which is the lack of trust in meaningfulness, making nothingness a god. It seeks to affirm "meaningfully" that the world is meaningless and that nothingness ultimately prevails. Nihilism says there is a hole at the bottom of the Sea of Reality and all the meaning and value, if they ever existed, have run out.

Since reality, including the reality of ourselves, exists, we must acknowledge and work within the values of our environment, including our own human nature, in order for nihilism to be expressed. This means there can be no pure nihilism. It can only exist in a subversive form which unwillingly reveals the meaningfulness and value it professes to deny. The very effort expended in defining and proclaiming nihilism is an undeniable witness to the *meaningfulness* of language and the *value* of communication.

The logical inconsistency of any system that works within something which is not supposed to exist is obvious. We can understand this model more clearly and compassionately when we recognize it as an expression of hopelessness and despair from those who approach their finitude, failures, and eventual death without faith.

The Sophists, the Marquis de Sade, Nietzsche, Heidegger, Camus, and Andy Warhol have all expressed their own version of nihilism. It runs rampant through much of our contemporary culture.

The Face in the Mirror

Nihilism grows out of one's own personal feeling of hopelessness. As Helmut Thielicke explained,

> the real nihilist is frequently a man who is wallowing in his wounds in a self-tormenting masochism. He does not keep silent about his dreadful secret; he talks about it. And he talks about it with exclamation points and with a smile that one may well dread. He gazes into the abyss until the abyss gazes into him; he is intoxicated by its vertiginous fascination. He actually seeks out the lonely, echoing mountain walls from which he hears the echo of the agonizing mockery of his own laughter.[4]

Most of us may never experience such profound despair; yet this nihilistic threat is never far away.

People are, in fact, nihilists if they revel in the irrationality of the words and rhythms of sensational music. If they seek to run from themselves and the meaningfulness of personal relationships by immersing themselves in the crowd. If they surrender to the mediocrity of the media. If they become obsessed with possessing things—or people. If they dull their awareness of responsibility with drugs. If they become preoccupied with sex as merely technique. If they succumb to the absurdities of pessimistic humor. Or drown their longings for excellence in the comfort and monotony of an occupation beneath their ability. In a word, a nihilist is anyone at any time who does not live as though life is *worth* living and worth living *well!*

If, on the other hand, people get up in the morning, nourish and exercise their bodies, and admit either consciously or unconsciously that suicide is no viable option for those endowed with life in a world with so much to be experienced, they refute nihilism.

God *in* the Darkness

The Christian faith goes much further. The good news of the gospel is that when we confront irrational, insurmountable challenges, whether anxiety about the unknown or fears in the face of genuine dangers, we may follow our Lord who has been there before. Like Moses, we can draw near to "the thick darkness where God was" (Ex. 20:21). And Christ made a way for our faith even in the hours of excruciating agony on the cross. He cried out, "My God, my God, why have you forsaken me?" (Mark 15:34). He confronted meaninglessness head-on but did not surrender to despair. He rather prayed to His Father—our Father—and in the language of the Scripture (Ps. 22:1). In the midst of the most undeserved and senseless suffering, the bond between the Son and His Heavenly Father remained firm and unbreakable. This is tenderly confirmed when, as the echoes of His cry faded away, Christ met death with a childlike prayer which He may have learned at Mary's knee, "Father into your hands I commit my spirit!" (Luke 23:46). This is our answer to those who believe in nothingness!

Lost in the Crowd

When I was a university student, Charles Wells, a Christian journalist, told us of viewing a mass youth demonstration in Moscow's Red Square. Thousands of young people marched in deep snow, locked arm-in-arm, shouting: "We may be cold and hungry now, but we are changing the world!" In many ways this Communist prediction has come true.

I was in Moscow recently and visited the expansive Exhibition of Economic Achievement. Dozens of imposing buildings have been given to the Soviet government by countries politically and economically aligned with the Marxist system. In many of these buildings, vast world maps hang facing the entrance. A tiny red dot lights up at Leningrad, 1917, and then lights splash across the map, bathing half the world in red.

The Countdown

Many Christians throughout the world have already had tragic encounters with Communism as a secular faith and experienced its godless duplicity and cruelty. The rest of us should never doubt that our confrontation with this oppressive system will come. And while we may be annoyed at the attempt here to examine some of the perplexities of the Marxist philosophy, just remember that the Marxists do not balk at these difficulties. They believe their mission is to understand and apply this philosophy as they conquer the world!

Taking Philosophy Seriously

Although varieties of Communism exist, this discussion will focus upon its classical Marxist expression, as it relates to the Christian faith. Marxist Communism is more accurately called dialectical materialism. Its adherents believe that matter, particularly in its economic expressions, is *dynamically* in *process* of moving society toward Utopian equality.

As a student, Karl Marx was enamored with George Friedrich Hegel's philosophy. Hegel taught that society, indeed the universe itself, was being moved by our logical patterns of thinking toward idealistic perfection. He believed that when the mind had a thought or *thesis*, this thought was put over against another thought which challenged the original thought, or was its *antithesis*. In the dialectical dynamic process of thinking, these two thoughts were blended into a third thought, which became a *synthesis*. Since Hegel believed that all of *reality* was involved in this mental process, he developed and elaborate system to explain how history, culture, art, religion, and philosophy were moving toward harmony in an idealistic realm of Absolute Spirit.

Fruit Basket Turnover

Karl Marx was intrigued with these Hegelian thought patterns but vehemently rejected Hegel's idealism. "The philosophers have only *interpreted* the world in various ways," Marx accused. "The point is, to *change* it."[5] He boasted of turning Hegel's idealistic triangle upside down, or rather *right side up*, and placing the dialectical process on a firm materialistic foundation, for he believed *economic* factors, not ideas, determine history.

Marx taught that the possession of private property was wrong. It created greed which caused those who owned property and the means of production to exploit the working people. Therefore, according to Marx, the bourgeoisie, or "the haves," would continue to increase in wealth and power. The proletariat working class, or the "have-nots," would continue to own less and less. Eventually, as the alienation between the wealthy and the poor increased, the economically determined revolution or revolutions would come, ushering in the classless society.

The Opium of the People

Marx rejected religion because it was supported and controlled by the bourgeoisie. It was used by those in power to nurture a spirit of submission in the lower classes. Marx made his desire for the elimination of religion very clear:

> Religion is the sigh of the oppressed creature, the heart of the heartless world, as it is the spirit of spiritless conditions. It is the *opium* of the people.
>
> The abolition of religion as people's *illusory* happiness is the demand for their real happiness.[6]

Although today some limited concessions are granted to traditional Christian churches in the Soviet Union, and atheistic control is occasionally relaxed for propaganda purposes, this declaration from Marx remains the official policy.

The authorities at the border would not let me take my personal Bible into the Soviet Union! And my guide through one of the former churches on the Kremlin grounds pointed to a large dramatic mural of the last judgment and bitterly observed: "This is the way the Czars and church leaders kept the people in fear and submission before the revolution." She also smugly pointed out that the brick walls of the Orthodox monastery we visited on the outskirts of Moscow had the same architectural designs as the walls of the Czar's Kremlin. The tyrants supported the church.

Unpaid Debts

Marxism has a point in speaking against economic injustice and the subjugation of the poor. Its secular efforts to eliminate racial barriers and strengthen solidarity and communion among individuals by stressing the significance of society might also have value. Its confidence of purpose in history may be commended, though this is no doubt largely borrowed from Marx's Jewish heritage and the biblical confidence of God's involvement in history.

But can any of these values simply evolve out of a materialistic economic determinism? Can matter alone, and economic conflict, even if it issues in revolution, really produce social equality and harmony? These contradictions caused Bertrand Russell to declare: "Marx professed himself an atheist, but retained a cosmic optimism which only theism [a belief in a personal God] could justify."[7]

One must also challenge the belief that any system founded on materialistic and economic *determinism* could ever conserve the worth of the individual and personal *freedom*. This is no mere internal theoretical inconsistency. The political record of Communism in depriving millions of their freedom in order to preserve the collective economic system is open—at least for the *free* world to see.

The Two Tombs

The crucial difference between Marxism and Christianity can be most clearly perceived when we ask the question, "What do you think about the Christ?" (Matt. 22:42). For a Christian, the *person* of Christ provides the norm for inspiring and evaluating life in its unfolding purposes. As long as Marxism allows a dialectical *process* to be the standard for creating and interpreting history, the value of persons will always be secondary and in danger of being lost entirely.

Even though Marxists take history seriously, their atheism rules out the possibility for any fulfillment of unrealized dreams *beyond* this world. They are surely among those who have hope in this life *only* whom Paul said are "to be pitied more than all men" (1 Cor. 15:19).

The contrast between the historical confines of Marxism and the eternal hope of the Christian became vividly clear to me one Easter in Moscow when I visited the tomb of Marx's successor, Lenin. We shuffled along in line with thousands down into the flower-lined, heavily guarded mausoleum. Lenin's body, with its faint pink lifelike hue, lies in a glass casket. Hands and face appear to glow from within. One stands amazed at the preservation process, realizing that Lenin died in 1924. The impressions of this perpetual funeral are haunting.

Shortly after leaving the tomb, I worshiped in the Moscow Baptist Church, sitting on the platform beside Michael Zhidkoff, the senior minister. He wrote two words on a scrap of paper, then leaned and whispered to me: "Try to say these words as you enter the pulpit." As I stood to preach, with Michael as interpreter besides me, I pronounced these words from a strange language, *"Khristos Voskres"*—"Christ is risen." Instantly, with conviction the congregation responded, *"Voistinu Voskrese!"*—"He is risen indeed!"

Marxism, whatever it may accomplish in history, will remain forever chained to Lenin's tomb while the church of the empty tomb moves, sometimes unevenly but always certainly, to meet its risen Lord!

Free to Be Me?

During the early days of computer programming, I enjoyed a television spoof of our overconfidence in cybernetics, the effort to solve problems and predict solutions on the basis of information from the past. A football game was about to begin. Thousands of excited fans in the stands waited eagerly as the teams and officials prepared for the kickoff.

The ball arched easily down into the receiver's arms inside the fifteen-yard line. The runner returned the ball a short distance, was hit hard by the opposition, and fumbled the ball. The kicking team recovered, but committed a foul after the recovery and was penalized. At this point, the referee signaled for a time-out.

Computer analysts fed this data into a memory bank which already contained vast amounts of information on each player, coach, and team.

In the next scene the cameras zoomed in on the scoreboard which was flashing the *final score*. Instead of playing the rest of the game, the score had been determined by the computer from past records and the opening play, and the game was over. Television coverage concluded as the crowd of losing and winning spectators slowly left the stadium

This method of analysis and prediction, though humorous here, can be projected into an imprisoning philosophy of determinism.

The Way We *Were*

Although we have considered several alternatives which people might *choose* if they *decide* to reject Christianity, determinism challenges the very conviction that we are *free to choose.* It may be defined as "the doctrine that an event is completely explicable in terms of its antecedents." A determinist holds that "given complete knowledge of conditions, one would have complete knowledge of precisely how a person will—indeed *must*—act."[8] It is as though we are *free* to be what we *were.*

Many types of determinism exist, such as genetic, physical or materialistic, social, and economic (as we have seen in Marxism). I have chosen to focus on psychological determinism as seen in the behaviorism of B. F. Skinner.

While Skinner denied being an absolute or philosophical determinist, he questioned the possibility of knowing and believing in the existence of a human self or soul. He almost scoffed at an earlier, less-enlightened time when we believed in human freedom and said that now science insists that action is initiated by forces affecting the individual and that caprice is only another name for behavior for which we have not yet found a cause.[9]

Dispossessed Persons

Skinner used language skillfully and often redefined terms, giving the impression he was *not* denying personality, freedom, or moral values. Yet his basic depersonalizing program can hardly be denied in light of the following manifesto:

> What is being abolished is autonomous man—the inner man . . . the possessing demon, the man defended by the literatures of freedom and dignity.
>
> His abolition has long been overdue. Autonomous man is a device used to explain what we cannot explain in any other way. He has been constructed from our ignorance, and as our understanding increases, the very stuff of which he is composed vanishes. . . . To man *qua* man we readily say good riddance. Only by dispossessing him can we turn to the real causes of human behavior. Only then can we turn from the

inferred to the observed, from the miraculous to the natural, from the inaccessible to the manipulable.[10]

Skinner's disparagement of the person as a self and as a free responsible agent is further apparent when he said, "A person is not an originating agent; he is a locus, a point at which many genetic and environmental conditions come together in a joint effect."[11] Skinner went on to explain that an organism becomes a person as it acquires a repertoire of behavior which is reinforced during its lifetime and that our behavior at any one moment is under the control of our circumstances.

Skinner might be commended for affirming a unified view of personhood which neglects neither our bodies nor our environment. He could also be appreciated for challenging the illusion that our emotional lives are solely matters of our introspective insights or attitudes. But he moved too far toward materialistic determinism when he maintained, "thought is simply *behavior,* verbal and nonverbal, convert or overt. It is not some mysterious process responsible for behavior but the very behavior itself in all the complexity of its controlling relations."[12]

Responsible Freedom

While we cannot claim that persons are *totally* free and unconditioned, we must oppose any system which undermines the existence of a *relatively* free and responsible self. We are, to be sure, a part of all that we have met, but we are not *just* the product of our heritage and environment. It is one thing to say that we are *conditioned* by others and the world around us; it is quite another to say that we have been *determined* by those factors.

Behaviorism simply cannot point us toward goals to be realized; nor can it help us select the social programmers or patterns which have the right to determine our future. In fact, the psychology of behaviorism at times appears strangely like those humorous characters in *Winnie the Pooh* who are looking for a "woozle." They wander around the same tree so many times that they become fascinated by, and at times even fearful of their own tracks. Behaviorism tends to become cyclical and self-defeating when it says that, since we can control some behavior through programming and experimentation, all behavior has been programmed and is thus not free.

Determinism is no new challenge to the Christian gospel. In New Testament times the vast majority of pagans did not believe themselves to be free. They feared that their lives and destinies were determined either by fate (which controlled even the mythological gods), by the ever-encircling stars, demons, or perhaps the burdensome weight of matter itself, or the flesh. The Christians brought good news to that fettered world when they proclaimed the resurrection of Christ —that no power, whether spiritual or material, indeed, not even death could enslave Him. God raised Him from the dead, "freeing him from the agony of death, because it was impossible for death to keep its hold on him" (Acts 2:24). If this risen Christ, "the Son sets you free, you will be free indeed" (John 8:36).

"Man Is the Measure"

Another alternative to Christian belief is humanism, which on the surface appears to be the most noble and attractive secular option available. Humanism, as we encounter it in Western culture, stems from Protagoras, an early Greek philosopher who declared confidently, "Man is the measure of all things."[13] Protagoras was, as we might expect from this thesis, skeptical about any possibility of knowing the supernatural. He confessed, "As to the gods, I have no means of knowing either that they exist or do not exist. For many are the obstacles that impede knowledge, both the obscurity of the question and the shortness of human life."[14]

This same negative attitude toward the supernatural characterizes modern humanism as well. Paul Kurtz, admitting there are many varieties of humanism, explained that two basic minimal principles are present in all forms. First, there is a rejection of anything supernatural in the universe and a denial that persons have a privileged place within nature. Second, there is an affirmation that ethical values are strictly "human" and have no meaning independent of human experience. Kurtz explained further:

> Most humanists take man as a part of nature. There is no break between the human mind or consciousness on the one hand and the body on the other, no special status to personality or "soul," and no

privileged or special place for human existence in the universe at large. All claims to unique human immortality or eschatological theories of history thus are held to be an expression of wishful fulfillment, a vain reading into nature of human hope and fancy. Nature, for the humanist, is blind to human purposes and indifferent to human ideals.[15]

Humanism, then, is an ethical philosophy in which human beings, as part of nature, determine and seek the highest values. It can be very optimistic about social goals, as revealed in Corliss Lamont's definition of it as "a philosophy of joyous service for the greater good of all humanity in this natural world and according to the methods of reason and democracy."[16]

Humanism may try to warn us against shirking our moral responsibilities if we rely on a shallow supernaturalism. On occasion it may seek to inspire us to courageous social action. But why does it? Or why should it? Many crucial questions are left unanswered by this system of values.

But *Which* Human

Which *particular* human or group ought to provide the ethical standard or norm for human excellence and social progress? Christians point to Christ as the one normative human being they would like to follow and commend to the rest of the world. Humanists must be content with collective values or norms which are often evasive and selected because of cultural and individual preferences. These humanist standards, once selected, are difficult to apply when one needs to determine the value of a single individual in relationship to other human beings.

Well might Pilate, in a characteristically humanistic stance, gaze upon Jesus and nobly pronounce, "Here is the man!" (John 19:5). But how can the humanist possibly set up general criteria to determine whether Jesus *or* Pilate should be the man to behold and follow? There were good *humanistic* reasons for Pilate to be rid of Christ in order to prevent an uprising in the nation which might have caused extensive harm and loss of life in that atmosphere of hysteria.

Do-It-Yourself Values

How can humanism account for the origin of human life and the appearance of personal values? Is it defensible to believe that thought, language, interpersonal relationships, art, and countless forms of creativity evolved from matter and human will alone? Are thought and will really no more than biochemical processes emanating from the liquid matter of the brain?

On the one hand, humanism claims to believe in the evolution of all values from nature; yet on the other hand, it teaches that whatever values there are in the universe are created solely by human beings. Julian Hartt was justified when he wondered how values can exist in a natural world or cosmos only because human beings have deemed them valuable. Hartt pressed the issue by pointing out that in humanism a person

> is an island of value in a boundless sea of nonvalue. To the universe it is all one whether he lives or dies. Yet, he [the humanist] says, this man is an organic part of nature: and thus between value and nonvalue there is unbroken continuity. Between mere behavior and the good life, perfect continuity; between electrical charges and syllogisms and symphonies, perfect continuity; between visceral tensions and Calvary, perfect continuity. But does perfect continuity mean anything more than *underlying identity*?[17]

The humanist needs the Christian belief in God the Creator, both to distinguish persons from nature *and* to hold them together in His redemptive love.

Give Up the Dream

The deceptive, impoverishing quality of humanism can be seen most clearly in its denial of any hope for immortality. It seeks not only to discourage the believer from trusting in Christ and His resurrection but also denies the value of any naturalistic *longing* for eternal life. Humanism proves to be little more than a pale, hollow exhortation to be noble, good, and courageous in an indifferent and decaying world.

A Broader Measure

The Christian, however, may look with joy toward Christ who is "the firstborn over all creation. . . . the firstborn from among the dead, so that in everything he might have the supremacy" (Col. 1:15,18). No, it is not *man,* but Jesus of Nazareth, the *God-Man* who is the measure of all things.

> For the love of God is broader
> Than the measure of man's mind;
> And the heart of the Eternal
> Is most wonderfully kind.[18]

Notes

1. Richard T. Garner and Bernard Rosen, *Moral Philosophy: A Systematic Introduction to Normative Ethics and Meta-ethics* (New York: Macmillan, 1967), pp. 141, 146, 149.

2. Epicurus, "Letter to Mernoeceus," *Extant Remains,* trans. C. Bailey (Oxford: Clarendon, 1926), pp. 127 *ff.*

3. William S. Sahakian, *Systems of Ethics and Value Theory* (New York: Philosophical Library, 1963), p. 38.

4. Helmut Thielicke, *Nihilism: Its Origin and Nature—With a Christian Answer,* trans. John W. Doberstein (New York: Harper and Brothers, 1961), p. 26.

5. Karl Marx, "Theses on Feuerbach," XI, *Writings of the Young Karl Marx on Philosophy and Society,* trans. and ed. D. Easton and K. H. Guddat (Garden City, N.Y.: Anchor Books, 1967), p. 402.

6. Ibid., "Toward a Critique of Hegel's Philosophy of Law," *Writings of the Young Karl Marx,* p. 250.

7. Bertrand Russell, *A History of Western Philosophy* (New York: Simon & Schuster, 1945), p. 816.

8. Horace B. and Ave C. English, *Comprehensive Dictionary of Psychological and Psychoanalytical Terms* (New York: Longmans, Green, 1958), p. 147.

9. B. F. Skinner, *Beyond Freedom and Dignity* (New York: Knopf, 1972), p. 14.

10. Ibid., pp. 200-201.

11. B. F. Skinner, *About Behaviorism* (New York: Knopf, 1974), p. 228.

12. B. F. Skinner, *Verbal Behavior* (New York: Appelton-Century-Crofts, 1957), p. 449.

13. H. Diels and W. Kranz, eds., *Fragmente der Vorsokratiker* (Berlin, 10th ed., 1961), Vol. II, Frag. I. as quoted by Emile Cailliet, *The Christian Approach to Culture* (Nashville: Abingdon, 1953), p. 121.

14. Diogenes Laertius, *Lives of Eminent Philosophers,* as quoted in T. V. Smith, ed., *Philosophers Speak for Themselves: From Thales to Plato* (University of Chicago Press: Pheonix Books, 1974), p. 61.

15. Paul W. Kurtz, ed., *Moral Problems in Contemporary Society; Essays in Humanistic Ethics* (Englewood Cliffs, N. J.: Prentice-Hall, Inc., 1969), p. 2. See also the definitive *Humanist Manifestos I & II, 1933 and 1973,* ed. Paul Kurtz (Buffalo: Prometheus Books, 1973).

16. Corliss Lamont, *The Philosophy of Humanism* (New York: Philosophical Library, 1949), p. 9.

17. J. A. C. Fagginger Auer and Julian Hartt, *Humanism Versus Theism* (Yellow Springs, Ohio: Antioch, 1951), p. 140.

18. "There's a Wideness in God's Mercy," words, Frederick W. Faber, 1862. Tune WELLESLEY, Lizzie S. Tourjee, 1878.

5

The Ruins of a Temple

When I consider the world's *religious* alternatives to Christ, I feel as though I am walking through the ruins of a temple. Overturned and broken altars bear inscriptions of truth and value, but the dominant impression is of a haunting, vanished presence due to our fall into sin. While this is not the place for an exhaustive historical and systematic treatment of the major world religions, any inquirer or defender of the claims of Christ needs to know why Christians commend their religion above all others. To answer this question, I will present a broad survey of some of the major models in the spirit of charity, yet with a firm conviction concerning the truth of Christ.

If religion is our way of *valuing* that which has *ultimate* worth for us—whether this be God, wealth, power, sport, sex, popularity, or privacy, we are all inescapably religious. Can any of us remember a time when we were not aware of an overshadowing presence which convinced us that we are not entirely our own? People have always wondered about the origin of life and love. Those in the world before us realized that they did not have complete power to determine their destiny.

Without Excuse

From these sometimes disturbing, sometimes reassuring hints, which appear to be universal, have come the religions of the world. John Baillie gave weight to this consensus when he concluded:

> It seems nowadays to be a matter of almost unanimous agreement among those competent to judge that neither history nor geography can show us any tribe or people which is devoid of all religious awareness. We know of no human society, however savage and backward, which

57

does not already find itself confronted with the divine. It may be a matter of dispute whether all peoples are aware of deity as personal, or even as spiritual, being; but it is not disputed that all peoples have such an awareness of the divine as is sufficient to awaken in them what it is impossible to regard otherwise than as a typically religious response.[1]

While historical evidence from the ancient past is scant and never beyond doubt, it appears that as far back as we can go in cultural anthoropology, human beings have always been conscious of the existence and claims of the supernatural.

Early cultures have left dim traces of their beliefs through relics of worship, sacrificial altars, burial practices, mythological symbols, and literature. The ancient Greek poets sang, "Zeus and Apollo are wise and discern the conditions of man."[2] Plato wrote, "All men, Greeks and Barbarians alike, think gods exist and behave as if they most certainly existed and as if no suspicion of their non-existence were possible."[3]

The manifold expressions of nature, guided by the creative seeking Spirit of God, converge upon our spirit and conscience and enable us partially but really to know God. According to Paul, every human being in the race is capable of knowing through nature that: God exists; God is one; God is personal; God is righteous; God demands our total allegiance. Unfortunately all have sinned against this light and are without excuse (Rom. 1:18-25).

The Bible, therefore, encourages belief that the various world religions (whether established institutions or merely fragmented intimations of the supernatural) are evidences that God "has not left himself without testimony" (Acts 14:17). We may appreciate the original inspiration for the religions of the world and their longing after God, but at the same time evaluate their ultimate worth in the light of God's fuller revelation in Christ.

Judaism

Since I maintain that Christianity is not merely an outgrowth of the Old Testament but its surpassing fulfillment, virtually everything I say about Christ is in dialogue with the Jewish faith. However, summarizing some of the most distinctive similarities and differences between the two religions may be helpful. Believing that God in many and various ways has spoken and acted in His revelation to and through Israel, Christians may be profoundly grateful for the lofty contributions of Old Testament revelation and religion.

We may acknowledge not only this preparation for the gospel but also Judaism's enrichment of human life throughout history. When it has been true to the noblest themes of the Old Testament, Judaism has given the world high personal moral standards, an emphasis on the value of the home, and a witness, even through many holocausts, for social freedom and equality.

Through Israel the world learned that God is the Creator and that He is one. The ancient Jews taught their world, which was willing to wallow in a pantheon of many gods without challenge or commitment, that Yahweh is the one true sovereign Lord of all. The Jew never tired of declaring, "Hear, O Israel: The Lord our God, the Lord is one" (Deut. 6:4).

But Judaism was surpassed through Christ and Pentecost when God showed that His oneness was dynamically interpersonal. Indeed, His threefold being revealed the ultimate ground for our own personhood, the model for all our relationships, and the basis for our life beyond death.

While Israel taught the world that moral failure or, more specifically, sin, was essentially rebellion against God's will as law, Christ revealed that sin was in essence rebellion against God as *person*. Christ taught that sin was not so much an external act as an attitude of our hearts. He internalized our understanding of sin through the gift of His Spirit and energized the dynamic by which we might overcome sin and accomplish the demands of the law. Paul explained,

> through Christ Jesus the law of the Spirit of life set me free from the law of sin and death. For what the law was powerless to do in that it was weakened by the sinful nature, God did by sending his own Son in the likeness of sinful man to be in a sin offering. And so he condemned sin in sinful man, in order that the righteous requirements of the law might be fully met in us, who do not live according to the sinful nature but according to the Spirit (Rom. 8:2-4).

Judaism has never really entered into this realm of the Spirit. Rabbis still teach that good works, suffering, and even one's own death provide salvation. For example, "Let my death make atonement for all my sins"[4] is a revered formula recited when a life is near the end.

The Need for Atonement

The Old Testament covenant can also be appreciated for its revelation of the seriousness of sin and the need for an objective provision for atonement and reconciliation. The old sacrificial system included the slaying of the Passover lamb by every faithful Jewish household, the high priest's slaughter of the bullock once a year on the Day of Atonement, and the sending of the scapegoat into the wilderness with the sins of the people symbolized by the blood sprinkled upon its horns. This system was transcended by Christ's death on the cross.

The basic difference between Judaism and Christianity on this theme can be illustrated by showing how Christ and the Talmud interpret essentially the same parable. An owner of a vineyard hires laborers at different times of the day and decides to be generous and pay them all the same at the end of the day (Matt. 20:1-16). However, those who began the day's work early, though they received what they had agreed upon, expected to get more and grumbled at the owner:

> "These men who were hired late worked only one hour," they said, "and you have made them equal to us who have borne the burden of the work and the heat of the day."
>
> But he answered one of them, "Friend, I am not being unfair to you. Didn't you agree to work for a denarius? Take your pay and go. I want to give the man who was hired last the same as I gave you. Don't I have the right to do what I want with my own money? Or are you envious because I am generous?" (Matt. 20:12-15).

The message is clear that salvation comes not because of our goodness or works, but because of God's sovereign grace. We should rejoice at His being gracious to others.

This same story in the Talmud concludes with its doctrine of salvation through keeping the Law. To those early workers who complain about unfairness, the owner replied: "This one has done more in two hours than you have done throughout the whole day."[5]

To Bless the World

It was a gracious day when God made a covenant with the people of Israel that they be His special vessel to bless all the peoples of the world (Gen. 12:1-3). God was not to be sought in nature, speculation, nor even in morality. He made deliberate and particular encounters with His chosen in history. This "scandal of particularity" gives form and content to our understanding of God and His power to deliver and redeem. When Israel takes this graciousness as its own racial possession, or tries to sustain its relationship with God through works, it fails in its divine mission. Paul grieved deeply for Israel when he wrote:

> Brothers, my heart's desire and prayer to God for the Israelites is that they may be saved. For I can testify about them that they are zealous for God, but their zeal is not based on knowledge. Since they did not know the righteousness that comes from God and sought to establish their own, they did not submit to God's righteousness. Christ is the end of the law so that there may be righteousness for everyone who believes (Rom. 10:1-4).

Now is the time to realize that "there is no difference between Jew and Gentile—the same Lord is Lord of all and richly blesses all who call on him, for, 'Everyone who calls on the name of the Lord will be saved'" (Rom. 10:12-13, quoting Joel 2:32). That God elected a people to be His servant we can acknowledge with praise. We are more deeply thankful, however, that His kingdom in Christ now transcends all national, cultural, and ethnic boundaries.

When the Messiah Comes

Israel's prophetic longing for the Messiah, perhaps more than anything else, saved the ancient world from total despair. Today, regrettably, the various branches of Judaism which entertain the concept of Messiah are still looking toward the future. Neither Zionists with their nationalistic hopes, Reformed Jews with their striving for moral excellence, those Orthodox who think of the Messiah as the people of Israel, nor even those who pray at the Wailing Wall of Jerusalem can rejoice that the Christ has come.

Although Judaism and Christianity share many convictions and concerns, there is a world—indeed an eternity—of difference between denying that the Messiah has come and believing that He has come, risen, and is here. Martin Buber personified the way Judaism and Christianity have drawn closer together in appreciation and affection and yet remain infinitely apart in ultimate allegiance. He wrote of both his admiration for Jesus, and his unwavering rejection of him as Messiah:

> I firmly believe that the Jewish community, in the course of its renais-sance, will recognize Jesus: and not merely as a great figure in its religious history, but also in the organic context of a messianic develop-ment extending over millennia, whose final goal is the redemption of Israel and of the world. But I believe equally firmly that we will never recognize Jesus as the Messiah Come for this would contradict the deepest meaning of our Messianic passion. . . . In our view, redemption occurs for ever, and none has yet occurred. Standing bound and shack-led in the pillory of mankind we demonstrate with the bloody body of our people the unredeemedness of the world.[6]

Sadly enough, then, many Jews throughout the world, along with Buber, continue to pray to their God "who rememberest the pious deeds of the patriarchs, and in love wilt bring a redeemer to their children's children for thy name's sake."[7] Oh, that these would hear Paul's joyful announcement in the synagogue, "We tell you the good news: What God promised our fathers he has fulfilled for us, their children, by raising up Jesus" (Acts 13:32).

Hinduism

Many insist that Hinduism is a philosophy, or several systems of philosophy in one, and not a religion because it does not teach the existence of a personal God nor does it have a doctrine of creation. Yet it is a religion because millions of people give their ultimate allegiance to its teaching.

World Soul and Persons *Are* One

The fundamental conviction which underlies every major Hindu teaching is that Brahman, the spirit or soul of the world, and Atman, the spirit or soul of persons, are one. This sameness of everything is sometimes illustrated by describing Brahman as the air on the outside of a jug and Atman as the air on the inside. The duality or twofoldness between Brahman and everything else is merely a result of Maya or illusion which is a harmful result of faulty spiritual perception.[8]

This principle of oneness of Brahman and Atman is devoutly maintained by many today who represent the modern stream of Hinduism. One of their contemporary devotional tracts reads:

> The self is never born, nor does it die, nor, having once been, does it again cease to be. Unborn, eternal, permanent and primeval, it is not slain when the body is slain. I am the self of all creatures, being their indwelling Spirit; I am also outside them, not being enveloped by anything. . . . Knowledge is veiled in ignorance, and thereby mortals are deluded. But for those in whom this ignorance is destroyed by the knowledge of the self, that knowledge, like the sun, reveals the supreme.[9]

While it may be commendable to recognize the cohesion of all reality, Hinduism blurs the distinction between the impersonal and the personal, between things and persons.

Some Hindus believe that Brahman has from time to time become manifest in personalistic gods, such as Kali, Siva, Vishnu, and Krishna. These avatars, or incarnations, are really just concessions to enable people to grasp the ultimate impersonalism of Brahman, which is higher. Even if one were to grant the deity of these various appearances, the problem remains: Which deity possesses ultimate authority and deserves absolute intelligence? This problem is present in all polytheisms.

The Wheel of Life

Another common feature in the many forms of Hinduism is the belief in karma. According to this doctrine, every deed, good or bad, will receive its legally deserved reward or punishment. Any fortune or misfortune which may come to an individual is the direct result of the good or evil the person has done in this or previous lives. Only through the realization of one's total identity with Brahman can a person escape samsara, the cycle of rebirth, and experience the total annihilation of personal consciousness which is Nirvana.

Salvation, or moksha, comes to Hindus, they believe, more through a contemplative realization of their identity with Brahman than through any moral, spiritual, or personal transformation. When the

Hindu grasps the insight that reality is essentially one and that all apparent twofoldness or duality—such as supernatural/natural, divine/human, spiritual/material, or individual/race—is only an illusion, or Maya, then individual striving ceases and the person experiences Nirvana.

Blowing Out the Lamp

The realization that the self is one with Brahman (the experience of Nirvana) is, however, never to be confused with the Christian expectation of going to heaven. Nirvana can be experienced here and now when one becomes totally selfless. The experience is so nebulous regarding the devotee's personality that the survival of any kind of personal identity in the present, or after death, becomes highly questionable.

This blurring loss of the person can be found also in the popular modern expression of Hinduism known as the Hare Krishna movement. Here, followers of the benevolent incarnate Krishna long to lose themselves in their most characteristic devotional practice, the chanting of a mantra. This is but the repeating of the names of Krishna in the following manner:

> Hare Krsna, Hare Krsna
> Krsna Krsna, Hare Hare
> Hare Rama, Hare Rama
> Rama Rama, Hare, Hare

By chanting these names they hope to be filled with feelings of selfless bliss contemplating only the glorious form of Krishna.[10]

Occasionally the participants will dance while chanting, thus screening out any competing thoughts or sense impressions. These procedures are believed to delight Krishna, who is said to be dancing on the tongues of each of the worshipers.[11] While the devotees may expect to receive some blessing from these ceremonies, the blessing is primarily in the world-denying experience itself.

The Self as a Gift

The real world has meaning and value for Christians because Christ has entered it. Our encounter with Him illumines and enriches our understanding of selfhood. Ian Barbour summarized the essential difference between Hinduism and Christianity on this point when he explained that for Hindus, "it is the self as such which is the problem, and man should escape the self by detachment from all desires and emotions, or by absorption in the divine." For Christians, he went on to explain, "Self-centeredness rather than selfhood itself is the problem, and love toward God and man is the true fulfillment of individuality."[12]

Hinduism is so individualistically oriented that it has nothing like a church to nurture and sustain its followers. One interpreter explained:

> The idea of the Church is essentially incongruous, and therefore repugnant, to the Hindu believer. The reason is obvious. Religious maturity in Hinduism is the result of individual achievement in self-discipline, toward which others like-minded can only help by the inspiration of example or through wise counsel.[13]

The concept of an involved community seeking to transform society is alien to the Hindu conviction that people are to seek and welcome their absorption into the all.[14]

How much more sustaining and delightful it is to believe that all who have not run from themselves and their responsibilities but have kept their faith in Christ will one day be able to exclaim, "I have fought the good fight, I have finished the race, I have kept the faith. Now there is in store for me the crown of righteousness, which the Lord, the righteous Judge, will award to me on that day" (2 Tim. 4:7-8). Imagine that! Christ's followers will never be lost in all encompassing Brahman but will abide forever with their personal God.

Through Thick and Thin

With his usual brilliance for clarifying complex issues, C. S. Lewis maintained that of all religions contending for our allegiance only two are worth considering: Hinduism and Christianity. Islam, he believed, is only the greatest Christian heresy, and Buddhism is only the greatest Hindu heresy. Lewis was confident that as a religion paganism is dead, and all that was best in Judaism and Platonism has been conserved and enriched in Christianity. He delineated between Hinduism and Christianity with this illustration:

> We may . . . divide religions as we do soups, into "thick" and "clear."

By Thick I mean those which have orgies and ecstasies and mysteries and local attachments. . . . By Clear I mean those which are philosophical, ethical and universalizing. . . . Now if there is a true religion it must be both Thick and Clear: for the true God must have made both the child and the man, both the savage and the citizen, both the head and the belly. And the only two religions that fulfill this condition are Hinduism and Christianity. But Hinduism fulfills it imperfectly. The Clear religion of the Brahmin hermit in the jungle and the Thick religion of the neighboring temple go on *side by side*. The Brahmin hermit doesn't bother about the temple prostitution nor the worshiper in the temple about the hermit's metaphysics. But Christianity really breaks down the middle wall of partition. . . . That is how one knows one has come to the real religion.[15]

Buddhism

Buddhism developed within Hinduism as a reaction against its speculative tendencies. It endeavored to make religion more a matter of ethics and experience while retaining the basic Hindu world view. It still holds that Brahman and Atman are one. The Buddhist often celebrates the oneness of all things and the unreality of human illusions in this kind of poetical refrain:

> Since everything is but an apparition
> Perfect in being what it is,
> Having nothing to do with good or bad,
>   Acceptance or rejection,
> One may well burst out in laughter.[16]

Buddhism also retains the Hindu law of karma, the samsara or cycle of rebirth, and the self-annihilating qualities of Nirvana.

Desire Causes Suffering

When, however, the young Hindu, Siddhartha Gautama Buddha (around 563-483 BC) had his experience of enlightenment, he became convinced that the greatest human need was not to contemplate the unity of all things but to relinquish the desires that cause suffering. He sought, therefore, to make his religion quite practical. In his first sermon at Benares he explained the Four Noble Truths:

The Noble Truth of suffering is this: Birth is suffering; aging is suffering; sickness is suffering; death is suffering; sorrow and lamentation, pain, grief and despair are suffering, association with the unpleasant is suffering; dissociation from the pleasant is suffering; not to get what one wants is suffering—in brief, the five aggregates of attachment are suffering.

The Noble Truth of the origin of suffering is this: It is this thirst (craving) which produces re-existence and rebecoming, bound up with passionate greed. It finds fresh delight now here and now there, namely, thirst for sense-pleasures; thirst for existence and becoming and thirst for nonexistence (self-annihilation).

The Noble Truth of the Cessation of suffering is this: It is the complete cessation of that very thirst, giving it up, renouncing it, emancipating oneself from it, detaching oneself from it.

The Noble Truth of the Path leading to the Cessation of suffering is this: It is simply the Noble Eightfold Path, namely, right view, right thought; right speech; right action, right livelihood, right effort; right mindfulness; right concentration.[17]

From the spirit and content of this message and from what we know of the life of Buddha and many of his followers, Buddhism sincerely tries to be a religion of compassion. A crucial difficulty arises, however, the moment we try to find the norm or example for right living. Though the issue is profoundly serious, Mark Twain's humorous thrust at the vagueness of a person's conscience might be appropriate to Buddhism. He said, "If in *doubt,* do the *right* thing."

But *Why* Suffer?

Buddhism's failure to provide an adequate personal example for right conduct can be illustrated by the famous mythological story of Buddha's encounter with the starving tigress. In one of Buddha's many earlier lives (according to some traditions he had no less than 550 previous lives), he was a young prince named Mahasattva. Traveling with his two brothers, he discovered a weakened beast which had recently given birth to seven cubs. The brothers agreed that the tigress could not possibly survive unless she found fresh meat and warm blood. The Mahasattva thought to himself that the time had come for him to sacrifice himself:

> For a long time I have served this putrid body and given it beds and clothes, food and drink. . . . Yet it is doomed to perish. . . . How much better to leave this ungrateful body of one's own accord in good time!

. . . Today I will use it for a sublime deed. Then it will act for me as a boat which helps me to cross the ocean of birth and death.

With a compassionate heart, Mahasattva asked his brothers to leave him alone for a while and he went to the lair of the tigress, hung his coat on a bamboo branch, and made this vow:

> For the weal of the world I wish to win enlightenment, incomparably wonderful. From deep compassion I now give away my body, so hard to quit, unshaken in my mind. That enlightenment I shall now gain, in which nothing hurts and nothing harms. . . . Thus shall I cross to the Beyond of the fearful ocean of becoming! . . .

Mahasattva then threw himself down in front of the tigress. But she did not move. She was too weak. As a man of peace, he did not have a sword with him, but found sharp pieces of bamboo and cut his throat and then fell down nearer the tigress and his flesh and blood were immediately devoured. Buddha concluded: "It was I . . . who at that time and on the occasion was that prince Mahasattva."[18]

While this story may evoke warm feelings of compassion toward nature and animal life, it reveals the tragic failure of Buddhism to provide a worthy example for personal religion. The Gospels are clear that when Christ shed His blood, it was to bring people into a living personal relationship with God Himself.

Blowing Your Mind

Buddhism's blurring of personal values in also present in Zen Buddhism, so popular today. A modern interpreter of Zen declared that followers need to realize that the true self is unattainable. However, he explained, paradoxically, that this "is a turning point from the realization that our True Self is unattainable to the realization that the unattainable itself is our True Self."[19]

Zen Buddhism encourages its followers to meditate on mysterious riddles in order to enhance a spiritual outlook on life. This type of conceptual puzzle is called a *koan*. Zen has more than seventeen hundred of these koans. One asks:

> Since you can make the sound
> Of two hands clapping,

What would be the sound
Of one hand?

By contemplating such a problem, the mind is supposedly freed from normal, logical, and rigid patterns of thinking. When the logic and dualism of our illusory thinking break down, then enlightenment, *satori*, takes place, and we are free to live life at its fullest.

The difference between Buddhism's asking us to deny our consciousness and thirst for life and Christ's invitation to deny ourselves, take up our cross, and follow Him (Mark 8:34) is crucial. We follow Him to a wedding and ask, "Is Buddha there?" Or is the occasion too fraught with desire? We stand by Christ's side, hear Him call a child by name and bring her back to life and wonder whether Buddha, if he could, would call her back to this tragic world. We follow our Lord to His empty grave and are stunned by Buddha's cold warning that we are not even to desire to participate in a resurrection life. G. K. Chesterton addressed these questions when he asserted, "We may call Buddhism a faith; though to us it seems more like a doubt."[20]

Islam

The name *Islam* means "surrender" to the sovereignty and will of God, Allah. When Muhammad (AD 570-632) appeared in Arabia, that society needed a prophet to denounce the shallow uncertainties of idolatry and voice a strong witness for the oneness of God. He established a religion, with its roots in Judaism and Christianity, that has become crystallized in the "five pillars of Islam." They are: the witness to God's oneness; scheduled prayer five times a day; alms giving; fasting, particularly in the month commemorating the giving of the Koran; and pilgrimage to Mecca. Occasionally a holy war is considered as a sixth pillar.

The Lost Father

Five times a day the devout Muslim will face Mecca and repeat the following prayer:

> God is most great. God is most great. I bear witness that Muhammad is the apostle of God. God is most great. In the name of God, the merciful Lord of mercy. Praise be to God the Lord of the worlds, the merciful Lord of mercy, Sovereign of the day of judgment. Thee alone

it is we worship; Thee alone we implore to help. Guide us in the straight path, the path of those to whom thou art gracious, who are not the incurrers of thine anger, nor wanderers in error. God is most great, God is most great . . . I bear witness that Muhammad is the apostle of God . . . May God send down blessing upon him and preserve him in peace. Peace rest upon you and the mercy of God.[21]

Here are noble themes concerning God's existence, oneness, sovereignty, judgment, and mercy. Our absolute responsibility to live in surrender to God is clearly acknowledged. Yet there are some profound limitations in this "witness." For example, neither here, nor anywhere in the Koran, is God called Father. We ask where we are to look for that person, place, or revelation which can clarify for us what the Muslim means by the name of God? And we are told to go only to the Koran which God dictated through the angel Gabriel to the prophet Muhammad.

A Character Witness

When we take up the Koran and read of God's arbitrary sovereignty and Muhammad's indulgent moral character, we are disappointed. We are told without embarrassment or confession of God's blessing upon Muhammad's sensuous self-centered life:

O prophet, we have allowed thee thy wives unto whom thou hast given their dower, and also the slaves which thy right hand possesseth, of the booty which God hath granted thee; and the daughters of thy uncle, and the daughters of thy aunts, both on thy father's side, and on thy mother's side, who have fled with thee from Mecca, and any other believing woman, if she give herself unto the prophet; in case the prophet desireth to take her to wife. . . . And thou mayest take unto thee her whom thou shalt please, and her whom thou shalt desire . . . and it shall be no crime in thee.[22]

This compromising of God's holiness and the spiritual endorsement of such an open sexual life-style is especially surprising when we remember that it occurs seven centuries after Christ. Nor has there ever been any official annulment of this passage in the Koran or repudiation of polygamy in the main stream of Islam.

While Hinduism and Buddhism mystically neglect this world and the course of human events, Islam has confidence that God does, indeed, act in history, a theme it largely inherited from Judaism and Christianity. However, Islam's belief in the possibility of a holy war is closer to the Old Testament than to the religion of Christ.

Even though Christianity has failed its Lord on many occasions in this area, the gentle spirit of Christ has always stood in judgment against violence and sought to bring His followers nearer to peace. However, the use of force for good causes, even for the spread of the faith, is clearly allowed and deeply embedded in the Koran (chs. 2, 48, and 66). These passages, as well as the pervading military spirit of the Koran, reveal how far Islam departed from Christ's example.

The Lost Son

Islam passionately rejects the belief that God could enter personally into history. The Koran teaches explicitly, "It is not meet for God, that he should have any son,"[23] a conviction which is written repeatedly around the Mosque of Omar in Jerusalem. This denial of any possibility of an incarnation of the Son of God shows not only Islam's rejection of Christ but also its failure to establish a personal norm for values in history.

The fact that the Koran even denies that Jesus was crucified is a further indication that Islam is unwilling to take the personal dimension of history seriously. One passage claims:

> And for their [the Jews] saying, "Verily we have slain the Messiah, Jesus the son of Mary, an Apostle of God." Yet they slew him not, and they crucified him not, but they had only his likeness. . . . and they did not really slay him, but God took him up to Himself. And God is Mighty, Wise!"[24]

Islamic scholars are divided in their interpretations of this theme. Some say it means the Jews did not crucify Jesus but God did. Others believe that the sovereignty of God would not have allowed Jesus to be killed. Others hold that He escaped the cross and someone else was crucified in His place. The consensus seems to be, however, that Jesus was not crucified but that God carried Him away to safety in the heavens. The result of these cumulative denials is that Islam through the centuries has stressed God's sovereignty and His action within history, but not as the action of divine goodness nor the revelation and giving of personal suffering love.

So Near and Yet So Far

The differences between Islam and Christianity can be seen in Alfred Guillaume's projection of what Islam would strike from the Apostles' Creed. The phrases in parentheses and italics are not valid according to Islam:

> I believe in God (*the Father*)
> Almighty, Maker of heaven and earth:
> And in Jesus Christ
> (*His only Son our Lord*)
> Who was conceived of the Holy Ghost
> Born of the Virgin Mary
> (*Suffered under Pontius Pilate,*
> *Was crucified*
> *Dead and buried.*
> *He descended into Hell.*
> *The third day he rose again from the dead*).
> He ascended into heaven
> (*And sitteth on the right hand of God the*
> *Father almighty*).
> From thence he shall come
> (*To judge the quick and the dead*).
> I believe in the Holy Ghost
> (*The Holy Catholic Church,*
> *The Communion of Saints*),
> The forgiveness of sins,
> The resurrection of the body
> And the life everlasting.[25]

Even though it might appear that there are many agreements between these two faiths, the references to God or the Holy Spirit without the sonship or deity of Christ mean that God cannot be understood as thoroughly personal. God will always tend to be merely a sovereign force for these who reject the incarnation of Christ.

The Holy Spirit in Islam might be an instrument of God but can hardly be the person of God Himself as Spirit. Only in the Spirit's relationship to Christ can we know Him as personal Spirit. Christians who take seriously Christ's commission to take the gospel into all the world in the "name of the Father and of the Son and of the Holy Spirit" (Matt. 28:19) are right both theologically and logically to believe that only those who honor this threefold personal name truly know and worship God.

Composite Religion

Many today feel that none of these religions alone is adequate to meet all their religious needs. They, therefore, try to select the better elements in all religions and give allegiance and practice to a religious pluralism or composite religion. Believing that most religions possess truth and value, they hope to avoid being intolerant of other faiths. They also want to rise above the limitations of a particular religious institution.

Homogenized Religions

Historian Arnold Toynbee, after a lifetime of surveying the religions of the world, came to believe that one religion could be formed which should include these major teachings: (1) There is a presence in the universe that is spiritually greater than each person. (2) In human life, knowledge is not an end in itself, but is a means to action. (3) Each individual's goal is to seek communion with the presence behind all things and to seek it with the aim of achieving harmony with this absolute spiritual reality. (4) A human self cannot be brought into harmony with absolute reality unless it can get rid of its innate self-centeredness. This is the hardest task that persons can set for themselves. (5) Absolute reality has both an impersonal and a personal aspect. (6) The personal aspect of absolute reality must be good as well as omnipotent.[26]

Alongside these cardinal teachings, Toynbee proposed a cosmopolitan liturgy, or order of devotion, which he believed enshrines all the essential elements for true worship. He praised and invoked the blessing of many deities, including Jesus Christ, Osiris, Balder, Buddha, Mother Mary, Saint Michael, and Mithras. The vaporous content of this worship is characterized by the frequent hollow refrain: "Hear us, by whatsoever name we bless Thee."[27]

Such a collage of religions has many problems, including the impossibility of combining so many different views of ultimate reality, ethics, and salvation. The greatest weakness, however, is the loss of any historical focus or norm for such a faith. Must we not be continually asking to what or to whom we really owe our greatest allegiance?

True, some may contend that the historical manifestation of a religion can easily detract from its universal and eternal significance. But the essence of the Christian faith is that God became flesh in Christ in such a way as to anchor His revelation in history, and at the same time demonstrate its universal and eternal relevance.

One Of a Kind

G. Ernest Wright believed that the fact that God acted in history sets apart the faith of the Old Testament from its surrounding religions and cultures. He explained that religious literature produced in all those countries—India, China, Persia—is very different from the Bible.

> The Veda of Hinduism, the Pali literature of Buddhism, the Confucian Classics, and the Avesta of Zoroastrianism are all composed for the most part of liturgical material and especially of *teachings* on a great variety of subjects. None of them has any particular historical interest. Even the Koran of Islam . . . is chiefly a series of teachings from the auditions and the visions of the prophet Mohammad.[28]

If the Old Testament faith was unique because God acted in history, this may be claimed even more distinctly for the religion of the one who was "crucified under Pontius Pilate." This willingness of God to allow His revelation and self-giving to become the dateable stuff of human experience gives the Christian faith its personal content and preserves it from a shallow pluralistic relativism. The naive complacency of our age toward combining elements from many religions needs G. K. Chesterton's warning: "Nobody understands the nature of the Church, or the ringing note of the creed descending from antiquity, who does not realize that the whole world once very nearly died of broadmindedness and the brotherhood of all religions."[29]

Let's Meet, Everywhere

Christianity dreams of uniting the human race under the lordship of Christ. But a religion like Toynbee suggested is so inclusive and uncommitted to any particular historical demonstration of the truth that it could not accomplish this purpose. I share D. T. Niles's concern when he said, "The Universalism for which Toynbee pleads atomizes the human community. Each can go his own way to God, and therefore, one can find God without finding his brother."[30] Very simply, Toynbee invited the world to join hands without telling us *where* to meet. Christians believe that God has shown His love to the world in Christ by providing "one Lord, one faith, one baptism" (Eph. 4:5). The uniqueness of this revelation and giving of Christ in history is far more gracious and unifying than the apparent freedom of a common search.

Room at the Top

Recently in New Zealand I met Sir Edmund Hillary and visited with him in his home. He was the first to climb Mount Everest, the world's highest peak. To be in the presence of one who has ascended to the rarefied atmosphere of 27,900 feet was inspiring. Hillary told about that expedition. They left their night camp in a temperature hovering around minus 27 degrees Celsius. He and Tenzing, his Tibetan companion, had a painful fight for every inch through chiseled ice, every breath the result of a determined gasp. In his diary he recorded:

> I continued on, cutting steadily and surmounting bump after bump and cornice after cornice looking eagerly for the summit. It seemed impossible to pick it and time was running out. Finally I cut around the back of an extra large hump and then on a tight rope from Tenzing I climbed up a gentle snow ridge to its top. Immediately it was obvious that we had reached our objective. It was 11:30 a.m. and we were on top of Everest!
>
> To the north an impressive corniced ridge ran down to the East Rongbuk glacier . . . we were looking down on the North Col and Changtse. The West ridge dropped away in broad sweeps and we had a great view . . . far below us [the peaks] to the east looking considerably less impressive than I had ever seen them. . . . It was a great moment![31]

We may make our way through the mountain peaks of the religions of the world and strive to reach the top only to realize to our amazement that when we accept Christ we are already there! When we meet Him, we may gaze below to the other religions of the world and have no desire to descend to those lower mountains which are "considerably less impressive." We have arrived, not through our own striving as Hillary did, but because on Mount Calvary Christ came down to lift us up.

Notes

1. John Baillie, *Our Knowledge of God* (London: Oxford University Press, 1939), p. 6.

2. "Oedipus the King," *The Oedipus Plays of Sophocles,* trans. Paul Roche (New York: Mentor Books, 1958), p. 43.

3. Plato, *Laws,* trans. A. E. Taylor (London: Dent & Sons, 1934), Bk. X, 886, p. 275.

4. Kaufmann Kohler, "Atonement," *The Jewish Encyclopedia* (New York: Funk & Wagnalls, 1902), II: 279, quoting Berakot Talmud 60a and Sanhedrin Talmud vi.2.

5. Hermann Strack and Paul Billerbeck, *Exkurse zu Einzelnen Stellen des Neuen Testaments* (Muenchen: Beck Verlag, 1928), 4.1:493.

6. Martin Buber as quoted in Stephen Neill, *Christian Faith and Other Faiths* (Downers Grove, Ill.: InterVarsity, 1984), p. 50.

7. *Festival Players* (New York: Bloch, 1924), p. 11.

8. Sankara Karya, *Vedanta-Sutras,* trans. George Thibaut, *Sacred Books of the East,* ed. Max Mueller (Oxford: Clarendon, 1890), 34, I.I.5:2-53.

9. "The Supreme Self and the Body," a bulletin of the Vedanta Society of Northern California, quoted in Joseph R. Estes, *Worship in Non-Christian Religions* (Atlanta: Home Mission Board of the SBC, 1968), pp. 12-13.

10. "A Short Statement of the Philosophy of Krsna Consciousness," *Back to the Godhead* II; No. 7, 1976, 1.

11. J. Stillson Judah, *Hare Krishna and the Counterculture* (New York: John Wiley and sons, 1974), p. 50.

12. Ian Barbour, *Issues in Science and Religion* (Englewood Cliffs, N. J.: Prentice-Hall, 1966), p. 234.

13. P. D. Devanandan, *The Gospel and Renascent Hinduism* (London: SCM, 1959), p. 37.

14. Ibid.

15. C. S. Lewis, "Christian Apologetics," *God in the Dock* (Grand Rapids: Eerdmans, 1970), pp. 102-103.

16. Longchenpa, *Crystal Mirror* IV.

17. *Mahavagga* i.1, 2.

18. *Suvarnaprabhasa,* Trans, Conze, p. 206 *ff,* quoted in John Bowker, *Problems of Suffering* in Religions of the World (Cambridge: University Press, 1970), pp. 263-264.

19. Masao Abe, "Zen is not a Philosophy, but , . . ." *Theologische Zeitschrift*, Jahrgang 33, Heft 5 (September/Oktober, 1977), p. 264.

20. G. K. Chesterton, *The Everlasting Man* (London: Hodder and Stoughton, 1947), p. 279.

21. Neill, pp. 78-79.

22. *The Koran*, trans. George Sale (Philadelphia: Lippincott, 1913), XXXIII, pp. 348-349.

23. Ibid, Ch. XIX, p. 251.

24. "Medina," *The Koran*, trans. J. M. Rodwell (New York: Dutton, 1909), v. 57, p. 427.

25. Alfred Guillaume, *Islam* (London: Pelican Books, 1956), p. 194.

26. Arnold Toynbee, *An Historian's Approach to Religion* (New York: Oxford University Press, 1956), pp. 274-278.

27. Ibid.

28. G. E. Wright, *God Who Acts* (London: SCM, 1956), p. 57.

29. Chesterton, p. 206.

30. D. T. Niles, *We Know in Part* (Philadelphia: Westminster, 1964), p. 120.

31. Edmund Hillary, *Nothing Venture, Nothing Win* (Auckland: Hodder and Stoughton, 1975), p. 160.

6

The Flickering Lamps of Nature and Reason

Yuri Gagarin, the Soviet cosmonaut, was the first human to orbit the earth. He announced while still in space that he observed no evidence for the existence of God. Science was finally disproving the religious claim that there is a God. We might ask Gagarin many questions regarding his disclaimer. For example, are physical visual methods alone appropriate for disproving the existence of an ultimate spiritual being? However, the most probing questions might well be, Did you find the original *cause* of this universe? Did you see the hooks upon which everything hangs? It has long been a naive and dishonest tactic for the unbeliever to say, "Build me a world, start everything in motion and I will be sure to find some problems within it which will disprove God as the creative cause of all that exists."

A greater wisdom resides in the testimony of John Glenn, the first American to orbit the earth. Glenn is a Christian layman. Not long after he circled the earth three times in *Friendship* 7, he led a Sunday morning worship in Little Falls United Presbyterian Church of Arlington, Virginia, where he and his family were members. He reminded the congregation that a light-year is light traveling twelve months at about 186,000 miles per second, about seventeen times around the earth a second. Then he quoted a government document he had been given when he was accepted into the space program:

> When we recall that our galaxy is some 100 thousand light years in diameter, the sun being an insignificant star some 30,000 light years from the galactic center, circling in an orbit of its own every 200 million years as the galaxy rotates, we realize that even trying to visualize the tremendous scale of the universe beyond the solar system is difficult, let alone trying to attempt physical exploration and communications. Nor is the interstellar space of the galaxy the end, for beyond are the

millions of other galaxies, all apparently rushing from one another at fantastic speeds. The limits of the telescopically observable universe extend at least 2 billion light years from us in all directions.

Glenn then asked if all this just happened? Did someone just toss up a bunch of flotsam and jetsam? Did that matter suddenly start orbiting all of its own accord? He replied, "I can't believe that's really true. I think this was a definite plan. This is one big thing in space that shows me there is a God, some Power that put all this into orbit and keeps it there. It wasn't just an accident."[1]

A Hook to Hang Your World On

Most of us never experience so dramatically our dependence on an ultimate cause. However, the issue of dependence is the same as when we sit in a chair and read this book. We are causally dependent upon our parents and our ancestors for our existence, but who or what was responsible for *their* existence? We sit in a chair made of products we did not create, grown or mined from a planet we do not sustain, whirling in a galaxy we do not uphold. Something deep inside whispers that, if our experience of dependence within this world is to make sense, some distant first cause must explain the arrival and survival of our existing world.

The crucial issue is whether our *experience* in the world makes sense. Meaning itself seems tied to our understanding of *cause*. The meaningfulness of language, for example, would be questionable if we were never allowed to reason that some things *cause* other things to happen; we may, therefore, *know* a fact or statement to be true. I may ask you a simple question, "Why did you come to my house today?" If your answer never hangs a hook on what really caused you to come to my house, but wanders aimlessly and endlessly on factors which merely *accompany* your visit, I must conclude that your answer is irrational and meaningless.

This kind of reasoning—that every effect must have a sufficient cause—lies at the base of all natural religion and forms the framework of our belief that God speaks through nature. The sheer fact of our dependency on things and circumstances which we did not cause cries out for humble acknowledgment of an ultimate cause. There might be a hypothetical and mathematical possibility of infinite regress, where the chain is *never* placed on a hook or the knot in things is never tied. Yet the counsel of Job seems much wiser; he encouraged us to trust in *God,* who "spreads out the northern skies over empty space; he suspends the earth over nothing" (Job 26:7). The fact remains that our experience of meaningfulness never takes place apart from our belief that we have been *caused* by one greater than ourselves.

One World

The New Testament concludes that since the world exists it has been caused and God is that cause. This belief can be seen in Paul's reasoning: "For the invisible things of him from the creation of the world are clearly seen, being understood by the things that are made, even his eternal power and Godhead" (Rom. 1:20, KJV). Perhaps because we know our evil inclinations and sins all to intimately, we are easily tempted to turn God into an object or a process rather than to acknowledge Him as the personal Creator who draws near.

Process or Person

Goethe portrayed our tendency to keep God at a distance with painful clarity in *Faust.* He described Mephistopheles' tempting Faust to take the biblical phrase, "In the beginning was the Word," and translate it, "In the beginning was the deed." The tempter realized that, when God is considered merely as some act or process, He is further removed from being considered a person who speaks His Word.

The reasoning from the existence of the world to God as the first cause who made it cries out for understanding of God's personal purposes with His world. Fortunately, at just this juncture, the redemptive action of God in history took place to provide the necessary basis for our knowledge of God as Creator. In our Christian experience, we learn to believe not only in "creation," or in some impersonal "process," but also in Christ in whom all things have their origin and coherence (Col. 1:17). We can say now with Martin Luther, "I believe that God has created *me.*"[2]

This kind of belief was experienced by the son of a Russian nobleman who estranged himself from his father by his frequent trips to Nikolsburg to study with the famous Rabbi Shmelke. Once when the son returned briefly after a long absence, the father challenged him:

"And just what have you learned?" The boy answered, "I have learned that God is the Creator of the world." In exasperation the father called for one of his most ignorant servants and asked him, "Did you know that God created the world?" to which the servant replied, "Yes, I know that." The son thoughtfully responded, "Of course, they all say so, but do they also *learn* it?"[3] The Christian longs to affirm the belief that God is his Creator and to *learn* it in trust day by day.

For the Beauty of the Earth

The world has come into being through a cause which the dependent causes of the world cannot explain. It also is designed wonderfully and gloriously. These statements demand faith, for many things in our world appear to support the view that our world is haphazardly moving on its own.

We readily admit that the world as we understand it is not perfect according to our desires. It contains many barriers to our present happiness and even the seed of our certain death. Yet the prophet discerned an overarching pattern of design and purposefulness and declared that when God "formed and made the earth—he made it firm and lasting. He did not make it a desolate waste, but a place for people to live" (Isa. 45:18, GNB).

The nineteenth-century hymn writer F. S. Pierpoint gave beautiful expression to the beauty of the earth and the appropriate human response:

> For the beauty of the earth,
>   For the glory of the skies,
> For the love which from our birth
>   Over and around us lies:
> For the joy of ear and eye,
>   For the heart and mind's delight,
> For the mystic harmony
>   Linking sense to sound and sight:
> Christ our God, to thee we raise
> This our hymn of grateful praise.[4]

Lock *and* Key

God is not only the Maker, Designer, and Sustainer of the world but also is the great Artist. He maintains the world by His power, and this He does *marvelously*. The psalmist exclaimed, "The heavens declare the glory of God;/the skies proclaim the work of his hands" (Ps. 19:1). The amazing fact is that men and women are so constituted that they are able to comprehend and correspond with the purposes of the world around them.

The Scripturese praise the grandeur of *nature*, singing, "When I consider your heavens,/the work of your fingers,/the moon and the stars,/which you have set in place,/what is man that your are mindful of him?/the son of man that you care for him?" (Ps. 8:3-4). The psalmist then rejoiced in the fact that we as *persons* can delight in this natural glory and participate vitally with it under the care of our Creator. "You made him a little lower than the heavenly beings/and crowned him with glory and honor./You made him ruler over the works of your hands" (v. 5). Nature and persons, therefore, fit together providentially like lock and key, like body and soul or brain and mind or, better still, like friend with friend.

Human Evidence

Human beings also provide evidence of their creation and design by a most intelligent and personal source. G. K. Chesterton portrayed the uniqueness and transcendence of persons in an imaginative way which shows the absurdity of the naturalistic evolutionary hypothesis:

> If there was ever a moment when man was only an animal, we can if we choose make a fancy picture of his career transferred to some other animal. An entertaining fantasia might be made in which elephants built in elephantine architecture, with towers and turrets like tusks and trunks, cities beyond the scale of any colossus. A pleasant fable might be conceived in which a cow had developed a costume and put on four boots and two pairs of trousers. We could imagine a Supermonkey more marvelous than any Superman, a quadrumanous creature carving and painting with his hands and cooking and carpentering with his feet. But if we are considering what did happen we shall certainly decide that man has distanced everything else with a distance like that of the astronomical spaces and a speed like that of the still thunderbolt of the light.[5]

Indeed, people are uniquely and intricately made with delicate bodies and mental and spiritual capacities. William Paley was justified in maintaining that the human eye should *alone* be enough to prevent anyone from being an atheist.

However, we human beings see, touch, feel, eat, and think. We also long for beauty, think noble thoughts, and relate with one another in love. And in many different ways, we yearn for God! In view of the striking agreement between nature and the fulfillment of human needs, this longing for God in our human nature is strong evidence that God is and may be found. C. S. Lewis reasoned along these lines:

> A man's physical hunger does not prove that that man will get any bread; he may die of starvation on a raft in the Atlantic. But surely a man's hunger does prove that he comes of a race which repairs its body by eating and inhabits a world where eatable substances exist. . . . A man may love a woman and not win her; but it would be very odd if the phenomenon called "falling in love" occurred in a sexless world.[6]

Long before Lewis, the psalmist based some of his confidence in finding God on this same principle. He asked, "Does he who implanted the ear not hear?/Does he who formed the eye not see?" (Ps. 94:9). Christ applied this logic in His teaching on prayer when He encouraged us to trust the Heavenly Father and asked, "Which of you, if his son asks him for bread, will give him a stone?" (Matt. 7:9).

The Highest Good

Nature speaks for God in the fact of the existence of the world. This encourages belief in a first cause and in the natural patterns of design leading to an understanding of God as the great Designer. Nature also speaks in our *moral* experience. Persons through the ages and around the world may differ widely in belief and practice of right and wrong. However, there is universal agreement that what is believed to be right really *ought* to be done.

We can get lost here in a maze of cultural and ethical relativism and believe that questions of right and wrong are completely determined by one's culture. The discrepancy between what people have acknowledged as moral law and their repeated failures to live up to these standards has always existed. What appears to be new today is that more and more people are surrendering to relativism and saying objective moral standards *do not* exist. This position is, however, accepted more *theoretically* than *actually*.

When at Baylor University, I taught a young international student who was not a Christian. He maintained vigorously in class that ethical standards were merely matters of taste. He held up his yellow pencil and said, "I like this color, and we all have certain tastes regarding right and wrong." We pursued the question, and we discovered that he believed he had certain objective rights should anyone want to impose *his* subjective ethics upon his new wife!

The Moral Law of Gravity

Cultural influences and psychological conditioning are obviously formative factors. However, they have never been able to destroy totally the moral altar within every human heart. There is a clearly recognizable consensus regarding basic morality. Individual, political, and perhaps national exceptions and deviations from the norms exist, of course. But throughout human moral history, people have believed that telling the truth, respecting the property, person, and life of others are *right* and whatever is degrading or threatening to another human being is *wrong*.

These basic principles are recognized and even sharpened by the United Nations. This is perhaps the most international assembly in the world today. By its charter and working policies, it condemns racism, combats sexism, and opposes dehumanization in many forms. It proceeds on the moral assumption that ignorance and hunger, especially among the disfranchised, are wrong.

Deep within the moral consciousness of every person there is, according to D. M. MacKinnon, a natural ethic complementary to, but distinct from, special divine commands. Within this ethic, moral oughtness provides the road to our growth as true human beings. "We rise to the full stature of our humanity, we become truly human by obedience to the dictates of the moral law. This is the broad high road to true health, individual and collective alike."[7] Not every culture at all times will adhere to these principles, but at no time will these foundations of human morality be removed and replaced by their moral opposites and contradictions.

The old sailor preacher, Father Mapple in *Moby Dick* illustrated this principle of morality in his sermon on Jonah. He pictured Jonah traveling to Joppa looking for a ship that could take him in the opposite direction from Nineveh and the will of God. He found one, went down into the cabin, and threw himself in his berth in exhaustion to wait for the ship to depart.

> Screwed at its axis against the side, a swinging lamp slightly oscillates in Jonah's room and the ship, keeling over towards the wharf with the weight of the last bales received, the lamp, flame and all though in slight motion, still maintains a permanent obliquity with reference to the room; though, in truth, infallibly straight itself, it but made obvious the false, lying levels among which it hung. The lamp alarms and frightens Jonah, as lying in his berth his tormented eyes roll round the place, and this thus far successful fugitive finds no refuge for his restless glance. But that contradiction in the lamp more and more appalls him. The floor, the ceiling, and the side, are all awry. "Oh! so my conscience hangs in me!" he groans, "straight upward, so it burns; but the chambers of my soul are all in crookedness!"[8]

Like this law of gravity, there is also a moral law in our world which we cannot escape.

Appealing to a Higher Court

The question now arises, *Why* should we attempt to live by these moral claims? To answer that we are to live in harmony with our cultural and moral tradition is inadequate. Traditions change from time to time between higher and lower demands, but the moral imperative remains committed to the highest personal standard. In other words, that which is *right* frequently challenges cultural tradition.

Nor will the answer of a merely functional or useful goodness be adequate to account for the breadth and depth of our moral experiences. We are often conscious of moral demands which go against the grain of our immediate comfort and seem to meet no current practical need. For example, how can we account for our feeling that we should provide for those who will come after us? Why *should* we plant trees that we will never eat from nor sit under?

The best answer acknowledges the divine nature of our moral obligation to others. This answer fully admits that morality goes beyond issues of cultural tradition, comfort, or convenience; it reaches into the supernatural realm. Since nature alone cannot explain our sense of oughtness, which is ever present and absolute, the reasonable answer seems to be that it originates with God. This explanation also gives support for the hope that right, having been done because it is right, will ultimately prove itself to be right and triumph.

Goodness Alive

This moral argument can bring us far enough to commend the existence of God as a viable reason for our moral experience. However, the Christian need not remain on this purely logical or formal level. For whether we are dealing with our encounter with the moral law through nature or the Old Testament, we know that the law was *given* but that grace and truth *came* in Jesus Christ (John 1:17). We may point to His sublime moral character as our ideal and receive the strength to meet His moral and ethical demands. We, therefore, agree with Brian Hebblethwaite's opinion. He said that when Christians claim the adequacy of Christian ethics they speak of an ideal—"the ideal of conformity to the one who brought the mind and heart of the love behind the universe into our midst, and of the spiritual resources for the eventual realization of that ideal."[9]

A vital clue to understanding Christ's ideal for our moral lives can be seen in His encounter with the rich young ruler. The young man said that Christ was "good" and even claimed to have kept God's commandments. Christ warned him, however, not to make goodness into an abstract principle nor to think of moral law as merely a list of moral propositions. He called for action: "Go, sell what you have, and give to the poor" (Mark 10:21; See vv. 17-22). He asked the young man, in other words, "Have these always been cold laws to you? Have you never really let God and His call grasp you and inspire you toward spontaneous exhilarating moral action?"

We have, therefore, in Christ our norm for moral goodness. The way He fulfills and transcends our ideas about morality provides yet another evidence for His claim upon our lives. The value of this kind of moral agreement between our sense of oughtness and Christ's fulfillment might be clearer if stated from the negative side. If the moral consciousness of the human race were to express itself in ways totally unsuitable and contrary to His ethical demands, would not this count *against* His being Son of God and Savior of the human race?

On *Having* to Dream

The early sailors dreamed of knowing more about their world. Something within them—whether the spirit of adventure, greed, or simple curiosity—kept calling them. After many journeys into the distance, when they put their charts together, they *had* to realize that the world is round. It wasn't that they just imagined it or wanted the world to be round; it was a necessary conclusion. They were not just thinking *about* the world, they were *in* it, sailing inescapably *on* its round surface.

Something about the world around us keeps whispering thoughts of a perfect spiritual being whom we call God. Whether we want to or not, we *must* think of Him. We are on, in, and surrounded by God's Being. Just as the world *is* round, God *is* here. And, if we make rational corresponding charts of our thinking about God, we *have* to acknowledge His existence and presence.

Beyond Compare

This kind of thinking unfolds in our reasoning. As we are involved in the process of thought, whether about abstract concepts (like hardness) or tangible things (like this hard rock), we make comparisons. These imply a standard of "perfection."

But from where, we must ask, does the standard of perfection come? Is it reasonable to believe that it is the product of our experience with imperfect things, or does it arise from our imperfect patterns and processes of thought? The concept of perfection just appears to *be there*. It is unavoidable. Even if we choose to reject the standard, we can only do so by claiming that our new understanding is "more perfect" than our former concept of perfection. This idea seems inseparable from our thought like our shadows from our bodies. And do not shadows mean that there are bodies and light? This inherent sense that a personal perfection exists somewhere inspires many people to follow their quest of impossible dreams.

The Correspondence Course

This longing for perfection, to be valid, must have some support from, or correspondence to, the reality in which it takes place. Otherwise our thought is sheer projected meaninglessness, like the echo in the forest from a fallen tree that never fell, or the image of a smiling Cheshire cat in a totally catless world, or looking for the meaning of this next sentence I will never write._____.

Since this standard of perfection necessarily exists in our thinking, the existence of God as a perfect being is implied. Otherwise our thinking would be greater than the reality in which our thought takes place. We may, therefore, conclude that, if our thinking has a rational correspondence with reality, God does indeed exist. We know this rationally from the very fact that we are unable to escape thinking about Him.

This argument, to be sure, has many limitations. It is abstract, and perfection needs to be defined. We might also question whether a perfect being is personal and graciously inclined toward us. Even so, the reasoning has inherent strength from the simple fact that the concept of God cannot be rationally avoided. The psalmist declared that the fool says in his heart, "There is no God" (Ps. 14:1); therefore, we may believe that the wise have good reasons for believing in Him.

The foolish are those who refuse to admit that they must think about God even to reject Him. They are like the villagers in the fable of "The Three Sillies" who reach into a pond with rakes, brooms, and pitchforks trying to dip up the reflection of the moon. God, like the moon, is there and reflected in our thoughts. No amount of irrational denial on the surface of the pond will remove Him from the sky.

Beyond the Shadows

All these natural evidences for God lead to this question, Which way does reality lean? We either encounter it as rational, meaningful, life sustaining, and value conserving, or not. We must decide whether we believe the reality which caused the world was benevolent and purposeful, or destructive; whether the patterns of nature are designed, orderly, and aesthetically pleasing, or chaotic; whether reality is interested in and capable of sustaining a moral law, or allows evil to exist unchallenged; whether our necessary thoughts and reality are correlated meaningfully, or exist in a vacuum without support.

Surely no one is naive or cruel enough to suggest that no problems exist in our world. Our limitations, pain, estrangement, evil, disappointment, and death are ever present. They arise both from the way our fallen world now exists and from our own fragmented understanding of it. However, even through these mists, the flickering lamps of nature give their evidence for God. But take heart! You are invited to "arise, shine, for your light has come" (Isa. 60:1). We need no longer remain in these shadows. Christ, the Light of the World, has come!

Notes

1. "John Glenn," *Parade,* April 1, 1962, p. 3.

2. "The Creed," *Dr. Martin Luther's Small Catechism with Explanation* (Rock Island, Ill.: Augustana Book Concern, 1922), part 2, p. 11.

3. James M. Robinson and John B. Cobb, Jr., eds., *New Frontiers in Theology* in *The Later Heidegger and Theology* (New York: Harper & Row, 1963), I:110-111.

4. Folliott S. Pierpoint, "For the Beauty of the Earth," 1864, *The Baptist Hymnal* (Nashville: Convention Press, 1975), no. 54.

5. G. K. Chesterton, *The Everlasting Man* (London: Hodder and Stoughton, 1947), p. 21.

6. C. S. Lewis, *Weight of Glory* (New York: Macmillan, 1949), p. 6.

7. D. M. MacKinnon, "Moral Objections," *Objections to Christian Belief* (New York: Lippincott, 1964), p. 12.

8. Herman Melville, *Moby Dick* or *The Whale* (New York: Norton, 1976), p. 45.

9. Brian Hebblethwaite, *The Adequacy of Christian Ethics* (London: Marshall, Morgan & Scott, 1981), p. 137.

7

The *Sure* Light of Christ

From the flickering lamps of nature we turn now to the evidences for the truth of the gospel of Jesus Christ "who has destroyed death and has brought life and immortality to light" (2 Tim. 1:10). When Christian begins his journey in *The Pilgrim's Progress* he encounters Evangelist who asks him, "Do you see yonder shining Light?" Timidly, the pilgrim thinks he does. Then Evangelist says, "Keep that Light in your eye, and go up directly thereto: so shalt thou see the Gate; at which when thou knockest, it shall be told thee what thou shalt do."[1]

Like Christian, we may journey into the faith with the light of the evidence before us. As we follow the gleam of Christ, we are clearly shown the way and may draw ever closer to that Celestial City which "does not need the sun or the moon to shine on it, for the glory of God gives it light, and the Lamb is its lamp" (Rev. 21:23).

It Is Written

While some people make sincere efforts to find meaningful evidence for Christ in secular history and literature, the fact is that we know of Him only through the Bible. We are wonderfully blessed, however, to find abundant testimony of Him in many reliable early manuscripts. Comparing the number of existing texts in ancient secular literature to the available documents of the New Testament, Bruce Metzger exclaimed, "The New Testament is embarrassed by the wealth of its material."[2]

The biblical manuscripts we possess are remarkably close in time to the events they record; some are dated as early as the fourth century. At least two portions of the Gospel of John are known through modern scientific methods of dating to be little more than a hundred years removed from the life of Christ.[3] On the other hand, 90 our oldest reliable manuscript from the historian Tacitus, who lived around AD 56-120, dates only from the ninth century AD.

We have also extensive quotations of the Scriptures in the writings of the early Church Fathers. These texts are on the whole so harmonious that some scholars believe that, if we were to lose all the New Testament manuscripts we possess, the quotations from these sources alone would allow us to reconstruct virtually the whole New Testament![4]

Christian scholars further encourage us that even when the texts of the manuscripts we now possess are not identical, "no doctrine of the Christian faith has been affected . . . for the simple reason that, out of the thousands of variant readings in the manuscripts, none has turned up thus far that requires a revision of Christian doctrine."[5] We can be encouraged, then, by both the quantity and quality of our manuscript evidence for the claims of Christ.

There is also good reason for trusting the historical and linguistic reliability of the New Testament. Interpreters, such as H. Riesenfeld and B. Gerhardsson, believe that Jesus employed the ancient rabbinic method of transmitting His teachings, emphasizing very carefully His words and the meaning of His deeds.[6] They believe the verbal impression Jesus made on His disciples and the trustworthiness of the formative insights passed on to the early church merit our confidence. This kind of evidence also corresponds with the belief that we possess the very words of Jesus recorded early in the Gospels before legends and myths had time to grow.[7]

The early dating of the New Testament documents does not guarantee the historical reliability of the writings. However, we have strong support for the close association between the first disciples of Christ and the Gospels. The Gospel of Mark was written, we believe, as early as AD 45. A tradition from Papias, late in the first century, says that Mark relied heavily upon Peter, a companion of our Lord, for much of the content of his Gospel. Vincent Taylor believed that about one-third of this Gospel gives evidence of direct dependence on the memory and testimony of an *eyewitness,* most likely Peter.

Again, Papias declared that Matthew, presumably the apostle, wrote down the "sayings of the Lord." These sayings must have become the basis for Matthew's Gospel written around AD 55. And according to the Muratori Canon, a companion of Paul named Luke wrote the Gospel that bears his name. Writing perhaps as early as AD 65, Luke claimed that his historical method of investigation was valid:

> Many have undertaken to draw up an account of the things that have been fulfilled among us, just as they were handed down to us by those who from the first were eyewitnesses and servants of the word. Therefore, since I myself have carefully investigated everything from the beginning, it seemed good also to me to write an orderly account for you, most excellent Theophilus, so that you may know the certainty of the things you have been taught (Luke 1:1-4).

John, writing around AD 95, left little doubt about his intention to provide a trustworthy Gospel:

> Jesus did many other miraculous signs in the presence of his disciples, which are not recorded in this book. But these are written that you may believe that Jesus is the Christ, the Son of God, and that by believing you may have life in his name (John 20:30-31).

These words increase in credibility when we realize that Irenaeus, writing about AD 200, claimed he knew the truth of this testimony from his teacher, Polycarp, who was a disciple of John, who had *seen the Lord.*

Assuming the letters of Paul were written within twenty-five years of the event of Christ's resurrection, as C. H. Dodd believed, their value as historical documents is enhanced. Paul's conversion encounter with the risen Christ occured very early in the history of the church, sometime close to AD 39. Either in Damascus shortly after his conversion or when he visited Jerusalem no more than ten years after the crucifixion, Paul learned of the unanimous agreement among the apostles that Christ's resurrection was true.[8] This probably lies behind his declaration, "Whether, then, it was I or they, this is what we preach, and this is what you believed" (1 Cor. 15:11).

The rest of the New Testament writings cluster around the same period as the Gospels and writings of Paul. No canonical New Testament books appeared later than AD 100.

We Have Seen

Another good reason for believing the early dating and trustworthiness of the New Testament witnesses can be found in those passages where eyewitnesses appear to be involved in the testimonies (Luke 1:1-3; 2 Pet. 1:16; 1 John 1:3; Acts 2:22; John 19:35; Luke 3:1; Acts 26:24-26). For example, Simon Peter demonstrated a bold confidence on the Day of Pentecost when he alluded to the agreement of his listeners by saying: "As you yourselves know" (Acts 2:22). Concerning this verse, F. F. Bruce explained, "Had there been any tendency to depart from the facts in any material respect, the possible presence of hostile witnesses in the audience would have served as a further corrective."[9]

Paul maintained in his great resurrection chapter, 1 Corinthians 15, that most of the witnesses he mentioned "are still living" (v. 6). Therefore, Paul proclaimed the risen Christ very close to the time of the actual event. This he did with authority, realizing that there were those alive who, if they chose, could try to contradict his testimony.

The Stones Cry Out

During Christ's triumphal entry into Jerusalem, His enemies tried to dampen the enthusiasm of the joyful crowd. But Jesus declared, "If they keep quiet, the stones will cry out" (Luke 19:40). In another way the stones of archeology give witness to the historical reliability of the biblical testimonies. For example, in 1961 archeologists discovered a stone fragment from the Roman theater at Caesarea bearing an inscription which they translated: ". . . Tiberium [a temple dedicated to the worship of Tiberius] [dedicated by] Pontius Pilate, prefect of the Judea. . . ."[10] This discovery gives supporting historical evidence concerning Pilate's role in Christ's crucifixion. Pilate's effort to build the temple to the honor of Tiberius is in keeping with John's portrayal of him as one who wished to prove himself a "friend of Caesar" (John 19:12-16).

Today there is little doubt that we know the location of Fort Antonia and Pilate's headquarters on the northwest edge of the first-century Temple area. I have been beneath the present level of the site to the expansive ancient courtyard where Roman soldiers stood guard and played games on the large etched markings on the stone courtyard. On this site I felt very close to the suffering Jesus, as I realized it was here the soldiers played their mocking games with Him. This is the ancient, accursed Lithostroton, or pavement, where Pilate "brought Jesus out and sat down on the judge's seat at a place known as The Stone Pavement" (John 19:13).[11]

Around 20 BC Herod the Great began reconstructing the second Jewish Temple in Jerusalem. This project had already been in progress forty-six years during the time of Christ's ministry (John 2:20). Israeli archeologists have excavated much of the walls and several entrances to this Herodian Temple. From the immense, precisely fitted stones they have uncovered, we recognize that the disciples did not exaggerate when they marveled: "Look, Teacher! What massive stones! What magnificent buildings!" (Mark 13:1). According to Raymond Brown, "The warnings of Jesus and of other first-century Jewish voices that all this could be destroyed seem more audaciously prophetic, now that we see the imposing solidity of what stood before their eyes."[12]

While these and all other archeological findings combined cannot stand alone in proving the Christian faith, they do encourage us to trust the scriptural witness to the redemptive events and message.

The Living Word

Although we have firm confidence in the historical character and reliability of the biblical documents, we must be very careful not to leave the impression that by itself the historical accuracy of the Bible guarantees or exhausts the vast wealth of the Christian faith. The Bible is a living Word which is the divinely appointed place where we may encounter the risen Lord.

In other words, the sincere and honest inquirer into the truths of Christ must be willing to allow the Bible to transcend language and point beyond itself to the place where Christ may be encountered as the risen and living Lord.

The Gospels do not claim to be memoirs or biographies. They never profess to be the writings of detached observers whose primary aim was to present mere objective accuracy. These documents were deliberately written as confessions of faith in Jesus of Nazareth as Lord! Their purpose is to evoke faith. When we realize this, we are able to move away from the arid plain of bare history and enter the realm of ultimate personal religious concern.

Our belief in the trustworthiness of the Bible rests upon a mysterious mix of external and internal factors. We can appreciate the way in which the historical references in the Scriptures match what we know in secular history. We are encouraged by the large number of biblical witnesses. This keeps us from fearing that the gospel was a hoax made up by a select few. The many and varied testimonies show that these accounts arose independently. Nevertheless, these witnesses agree on the most crucial facts and issues.

The Words Become Flesh

The New Testament writers demonstrated a willingness to act upon what they saw and believed. These writings are not mere dreams, traditions, or sermons; they are testimonies hammered out in the dusty arena of life and often sealed in blood. Christ creates new persons, transformed from their moral and emotional weaknesses into stable and consistent towers of strength. From this creative source, a new community—the church—arose; a new book—the New Testament—was written; a new day of worship—Sunday—was observed; a new order of worship—centered in Christ—developed; and a new life-style—service—began to grow.

We must now ask more precisely, What evidence do we have, both externally and internally, for accepting the biblical invitation to be a Christian? The New Testament gives many kinds of encouragement for trusting in the person and example of Christ. It sometimes defends Christ's relationship to Moses and the Old Testament law, to many Jewish traditions, and to the state. It affirms His bold teaching and practices about the sabbath and His stance on the role of women in society. However, the major streams of New Testament apologetics portray Christ in these ways: He is the Fulfiller of Old Testament messianic prophecy; He is the sinless or perfectly whole Son of God; the Miracle Worker; the divine Teacher; and, above all, He is the Lord risen from the dead.

Prophecy

One of the main lines of argument used in the New Testament to demonstrate the lordship of Christ is the claim that Jesus fulfills Old Testament prophecy. The writers firmly believed that Jesus' coming was foretold. They also believed that many details were given concerning the kind of Messiah He would be. Many of today's readers of the New Testament do not have exactly the same confidence in this kind of reasoning as those in the first century. However, they should at least consider the claims that Christ has fulfilled the *patterns* of Old Testament prophecies and longings.

On the one hand we may appreciate Christ as one who fulfills these promises. On the other, we should reverently refrain from viewing Christ as just a fact—albeit a dynamic historical fact—who merely fulfills the Old Testament Jewish expectations. Christ does fulfill the Old Testament and its prophecies; He also transcends them and recreates both the categories and the experiences by which He may be received and understood.

We must acknowledge the selectivity which faith employs when we speak of Christ as the one who fulfills certain conditions and aspirations. For example, Paul wrote in Galatians 4:4 that "when the time had fully come, God sent His Son." Through faith we can assume Paul was referring to the following facts: the Greek language was the universal language; the Roman Empire had established peace; extensive roads throughout the empire made travel easier; the Jews had been dispersed with their Old Testament faith and belief in one God; and many in the ancient world had philosophical aspirations. Paul Tillich understood this correlation between anticipation and fulfillment and wrote that the early Greeks were prepared for Christ. "Indeed, they unconsciously prepared his coming by elaborating the questions to which he gave the answer and the categories in which the answer could be expressed."[13]

Signs of His Coming

Jesus fulfilled the longings and aspirations of the ancient world; He also fulfilled specific biblical predictions concerning His coming. Matthew claimed prophetic authority from Isaiah's promise, "The virgin will be with child and will give birth to a son, and will call him Immanuel" (Isa. 7:14), to support the divine significance of Christ's virgin birth (Matt. 1:18-25; and Luke 1:26-35).

To believe the miracle of the virgin birth of Christ is for me a vital component of Christian faith. When I first became a Christian as a young boy, I did not even know what was meant by a virgin birth. Now that I understand more, I could not reject it in light of all the evidence in the New Testament and my experience with Christ. Yet the greater miracle is not that the Holy Spirit could bring forth God's

Son from a virgin womb, but that God's grace can forgive us and produce righteousness from an unrighteous heart!

The Messiah was, according to Micah 5:2, to be born in Bethlehem. This was acknowledged and claimed to be fulfilled in Matthew 2:3-6. He was to be a descendent of David, as foretold in 2 Samuel 7:12-13; Psalms 89:3-4; 132:11-12; and Daniel 9:25. These expectations were realized according to Matthew's genealogy (1:1-17); Romans 1:3; and Acts 13:7-23.

He was to enter Jerusalem humbly on a colt, as foreseen in Zechariah 9:9; even as it is described in Matthew 21:4-5. Christ's preexistence was intimated in Micah 5:2 long before it was declared in Colossians 1:17; John 1:1; Revelation 1:17; 2:8; and 22:13.

Prophetic Patterns

The most convincing kinds of evidence from prophecy, however, are those which deal with the broad *patterns* of Christ's life, ministry, and death. When, for example, the early Christians could view the death of Christ on the cross in the light of His resurrection, they were able to understand more clearly Isaiah's prediction that the Messiah would be a Suffering Servant:

> He was despised and rejected by men,
>   a man of sorrows, and familiar with suffering.
> Like one from whom men hide their faces
>   he was despised, and we esteemed him not.
> Surely he took up our infirmities
>   and carried our sorrows,
> yet we considered him stricken by God,
>   smitten by him, and afflicted.
> But he was pierced for our transgressions,
>   he was crushed for our iniquities;
> the punishment that brought us peace was upon him,
> and by his wounds we are healed.
> We all, like sheep, have gone astray,
>   each of us has turned to his own way;
> and the Lord has laid on him
>   the iniquity of us all (Isa. 53:3-6).

Reflecting on such prophecy, Paul proclaimed that Christ "died for our sins according to the Scriptures" (1 Cor. 15:3). Indeed, Isaiah 53 may be the prophetic background for the risen Christ's instruction to the disciples on the road to Emmaus in Luke 24:25-27, and for the messages in Philippians 2:5-11; 1 Peter 2:21-25; and Hebrews 10:12. In fact, almost the whole Book of Hebrews builds upon and serves as a Christian commentary for the Suffering Servant motif of Isaiah.

The psalmist longed for the Messiah when he declared,

> I will proclaim the decree of the Lord;
> He Said to me, "You are my Son;
>   today I have become your Father.
> Ask of me,
>   and I will make the nations your inheritance,
>   the ends of the earth your possession"
>
> (Ps. 2:7-8).

This promise was fulfilled and continues to be fulfilled in Christ as claimed in Acts 2:26; 13:33; and Hebrews 1:5; 5:5, as the gospel spreads throughout the world.

On the Third Day

According to New Testament believers, the Old Testament also prophesied clearly concerning the resurrection. One favorite passage comes from the Septaugint Greek translation of the Hebrew Old Testament, which the Christian writers surely possessed. It reads: "Therefore my heart is glad and my tongue rejoices; my body also will rest secure, because you will not abandon me to the grave, nor will you let your Holy One see decay" (Ps. 16:9-10). The New Testament witnesses in Acts 2:25-29 and 13:35-36 simply give the meaning of this Old Testament prophecy in the light of the marvelous and sure event of Christ's resurrection. This kind of argument from prophecy carried with it an immediate self-validating conviction.

Furthermore, the New Testament authors were convinced that Jesus predicted His own death, resurrection, and validation by the Father. From the time of Peter's great confession Christ told His disciples plainly He would be killed and rise the third day (Matt. 16:21). Remember He pledged the sign of Jonah that He would be raised on the third day (Matt. 12:39-40) and promised that in three days he would rebuild the Temple (John 2:18-22). He answered the high priest's question, "Are you the Christ?" with the confident, "I am, as you will see when my claim is vindicated and I am declared to be the Christ at my exaltation to the right hand of God" (see Mark 14:62).

Simon Peter could, therefore, preach that Jesus of Nazareth is both "Lord and Christ" (Acts 2:36): He is *Lord* because through His exaltation He fulfilled Psalm 110:1; He is *Christ* since through His resurrection He saw no corruption and thereby fulfilled Psalm 16.[14]

Servant King

Christ, as W. Sanday explained so beautifully, integrates and fulfills many different strands of Old Testament prophecy. The Messiah came both as ideal King and Suffering Servant. But these prophetic themes converge, not as we might expect, or would combine them artificially, but "in the sweet and gracious figure of Jesus of Nazareth —King, but not as men count kingship; crowned, but with the crown of thorns; suffering for our redemption, but suffering only that He may reign."[15] Isaiah prophesied that the Redeemer would come proclaiming good news, bringing healing to the blind, dumb, and lame (Isa. 35:5-6; 61:1-2). Christ understood Himself to fulfill these prophecies, and Luke added his confirmation to the testimony of his Lord (Luke 4:18-21; 7:20-23).

Christ is also believed to be the Fulfiller of those prophesies which speak of the New Covenant (Jer. 31:31-34; Mark 14:24); the giving of the Spirit (Ps. 68:19; Eph. 4; 1 Cor. 12; and Acts 2:33), and the sending of God's Spirit into the heart of the New Israel (Ezek. 36:27-28; 1 Cor. 14:25). The prophecy of Joel 3:1-5, concerning the coming of the Holy Spirit with power, was assuredly fulfilled at Pentecost, according to Acts 2:16-21.

Christ's fulfillment of these and many other prophecies is not just a historical fact which fits a theological system or argument for the verification of His claims. It is living evidence, which we may confirm in our own lives, that God keeps His Word. Rejoice, then, with Paul who stated that "no matter how many promises God has made, they are 'Yes' in Christ" (2 Cor. 1:20).

Miracles

Another evidence for believing in Christ, according to the New Testament, is that He performed miracles. The early testimonies were not planned to defend the belief that Christ's miracles really took place. Rather, they were offered in the simple childlike confidence that the miracles would validate themselves. The truth of the miracles would be proved by their spontaneity, integral relation to Christ's person and message, and ability to illuminate the mysteries and meaningfulness in one's everyday encounter with life and death. A. B. Bruce was, therefore, very near the biblical emphasis upon miracles when he said that people believe in Christ not primarily because of His miracles; rather, they believe in the miracles because they first believe in *Christ*.[16]

That You May Know

The New Testament at times warns against the shallowness of those who seek a sign or follow Christ merely in hope of receiving some personal gift or advantage. Nevertheless, Christ challenged His contemporaries to "believe the miracles, that you may learn and understand that the Father is in me, and I in the Father" (John 10:38). These works are portrayed in the New Testament to show Christ's supernatural power over nature. This power was shown in the stilling of the storm (Matt. 8:26; Mark 4:39; Luke 8:24), the healing of the man born blind (John 9), and even the raising of the dead (Luke 7:11; Mark 5:42; John 11). He has miraculous power over evil (Mark 1:26; Matt. 12:22; Luke 11:14; Matt. 8:28; Mark 5:1). He can also illuminate, provide regeneration and ethical transformation, and sustain His followers with an indwelling strength and presence (John 14:6; 15:3-5).

We are not only spirits but also flesh and blood and exist in time and space. Therefore, we may be grateful that God has been willing to give us some very tangible evidence of His power over the world and His personal concern for its redemption. Christ showed His power over both the physical and the spiritual when He healed and forgave the paralytic who was laid at His feet:

> Jesus . . . asked, ". . . Which is easier: to say, 'Your sins are forgiven,' or to say, 'Get up and walk'? But that you may know that the Son of Man has authority on earth to forgive sins. . . ." He said to the paralyzed man, "I tell you, get up, take your mat and go home" (Luke 5:22-24).

This physical miracle, like all of Christ's great works, pictures God's concern for the whole person—indeed, for His total creation. Surely we can understand if Christ chooses to destroy a herd of swine (Mark 5:1-20) or a fig tree (Mark 11:12-14, 20-24). After all, He made them. On those occasions He was only seeking to show forcefully the value of a person and the power of prayer.

And They Lived Happily Ever After

We may be sure that the New Testament witnesses to miracles were very close in time to the events they described. The reporters were many, of sound character, and willing to risk their lives upon the truth of their testimony. However, our acceptance of Christ's miracles likely will not be based on a critical historical study of the reliability and accuracy of the New Testament. More likely, belief will be based on our own approach to life and its mysteries and our openness to the spiritual and ethical claims of Christ.

We need to be sensitive to the mysteries of love, birth, the beauty and bounty of our earth, and even the way in which we exercise our personal wills over many physical objects. Then we can see plenty of evidence for the possibility, and even probability, of miracles happening in our world.

A person's belief that goodness has ultimate value and will triumph may give further encouragement to accept Christ's miracles. E. J. Carnell believed this theme so firmly that he even dared to write:

> If miracles are needed to ensure the final triumph of goodness, so be it. In this case, miracles are as much a part of reality as trees and rivers.
>
> A child knows that it is much more difficult to accept the defeat of goodness than it is to accept the reality of miracles. If good people do not live happily ever after, then what difference does anything else make? The most important thing has been surrendered. Death has triumphed over life.[17]

Christians are, however, not just engaging in wishful thinking. Rather, we declare that the miracles of Christ conform convincingly to our inescapable longings and beliefs about the ultimate goodness and triumph of life's personal values. Since we cannot avoid hoping for this victory, something in reality must create this desire and transform it into a belief. This belief finds its perfect expression and assurance in the person of Christ and His miracles.

The Moral Miracle

The most convincing evidence for believing in Christ's miracles is the spirit of *goodness* which they reflect. We are grasped by their sublime spiritual quality. Even Christ's enemies acknowledged this indirectly when they accused Him of performing miracles by the power of Beelzebub, the prince of the devils (Mark 3:22-30). This insight was perceived and developed convincingly by A. M. Fairbairn, who explained:

> But is not this the most remarkable tribute they could pay to His self-control? Would they have ventured to attribute to the devil in Him the power which they acknowledged that He possessed, if they had thought that His will was really devilish? Would they not have spoken softly and called Him by the gentlest names they knew, if they had believed that He incarnated malevolence rather than benevolence?
> . . . He is even to His enemies, more marvelous for the grace He impersonates than for the miracles He accomplishes. And this is simply saying that He was higher as a moral miracle than as a physical power. While the power may be great, the grace is greater, and men peacefully trust where under other circumstances they would have profoundly feared.[18]

This kind of ethical support for accepting Christ's miracles leads us to a closer examination of the unique and transcendent character of Christ as moral evidence for believing in Him.

The Wholeness of Christ

Christ's incomparable moral character and goodness provides for many people the most obvious and convincing evidence of all for believing in Him. His wholeness is transparent and self-evident to the believer; yet this is a difficult belief to explain. The *negative* claim, that He *never* sinned, can only be maintained in the light of the *positive* evidences recorded in the New Testament. It also takes faith to discern the spiritual motives and intentions of the human heart and not look only on the outward appearances. We must also realize that Christ Himself revolutionized the concept of sin. In fact, sin may now be understood quite simply as being unlike Christ.

One of the most encouraging signs for accepting Christ and His teaching as the basis for our understanding of sin is the nearly universal acclaim the world gives Christ's moral standard and example. Though many do not confess Him personally or theologically as Lord, few dare to condemn His ideals or find fault with His behavior.

No One Is Good—Except God

Christ claimed to be sinless when He challenged His opponents: "Can any of you prove me guilty of sin? If I am telling the truth, why don't you believe me?" (John 8:46). This claim was not compromised by His telling the rich young ruler, "No one is good—except God alone" (Mark 10:18). Christ was simply wanting the young man to interpret "goodness" in the light of his understanding of God; he was being challenged to accept the divine authority of Christ.

Many people, including Pilate who condemned Jesus, declared Him to be a "just person" (Matt. 27:24, KJV). The thief crucified with Jesus confessed, "This man has done nothing wrong" (Luke 23:41). Judas cried, "I have betrayed innocent blood" (Matt. 27:4).

Several passages in the New Testament present Jesus' sinlessness as an integral aspect of His sacrificial, atoning death. He is the perfect sacrifice for sin. For our sake, "God made him who had no sin to be sin for us, so that in him we might become the righteousness of God" (2 Cor. 5:21).

> How much more, then, will the blood of Christ, who through the eternal spirit offered himself unblemished to God, cleanse our consciences from acts that lead to death, so that we may serve the living God! (Heb. 9:14).
>
> For you know that it was not with perishable things such as silver or gold that you were redeemed from the empty way of life handed down to you from your forefathers, but with the precious blood of Christ, a lamb without blemish or defect (1 Pet. 1:18-19).

Christ's purity is also significant, according to the New Testament, because He is the perfect High Priest. "Such a high priest meets our need—one who is holy, blameless, pure, set apart from sinners, exalted above the heavens" (Heb. 7:26). This priestly work of Christ is enhanced by His involvement with us in our human situation, "For we do not have a high priest who is unable to sympathize with our weaknesses, but we have one who has been tempted in every way, just as we are—yet was without sin" (Heb. 4:15).

Christ's wholeness was no abstract concept projected from some idea of perfection. We know from His temptation experiences (Matt. 4:1-11; Luke 4:1-13) that His sinlessness was not untested innocence. "Although he was a son, he learned obedience from what he suffered and, once made perfect, he became the source of eternal salvation for all who obey him" (Heb. 5:8-9).

Friend of Sinners

Jesus' ethical perfection does not reside primarily in the fact that He did not commit sin, but rather that He turns positively in love toward the sinner. Gerhard Ebeling captured this lofty dimension of Christ's grace well when he declared:

> Sinless is not One who is for Himself while leaving others alone in sin. Sinless is rather One, who is *for* others to the extent that He takes on Himself what they are bearing. Sinless is not One, who is concerned or troubled about His own sinlessness. Sinless is rather the One who accepts sinners in order to liberate them from sin. Sinless is not One who condemns sinners, but One who encounters them lovingly. Sinlessness is not an anxiously treasured possession, but the freedom to surrender oneself defenselessly.[19]

Christ's wholeness is, therefore, not a negative legalistic purity which refuses, like many of the self-righteous, to become involved with us sinners in our need. It is, rather, a moral grace that is so spontaneous and self-forgetful in its goodness that it inspires and transforms. The character of Christ is sublime and unique as presented in the New Testament. Even one as far removed as Rousseau felt compelled to confess that if the testimonies concerning Christ's character were not true then "the inventor of such an image would be greater and more astonishing than his subject."[20]

The Truth

Jesus taught with a compelling and convincing "authority" (Matt. 7:28-29). His teaching on the transcendence yet intimacy of God as Father was revolutionary and unique. No one before or since has better integrated God's lofty ethical demands upon us with His command that we be gracious in love toward our enemies and forgiving to those who sin against us (Matt. 6:14-15). He taught about the promises, demands, and gifts of God, and He made the promises and demands Himself and, in the process, gave Himself.

We not only listen to a parable of the kingdom of God but also enter the kingdom through Jesus' teaching, as we accept Him as our king. Without neglecting the present, we hope toward the future not because Jesus explained it, but because He brought it!

Shakespeare's Portia was right to regret her moral impotence to follow her own good teaching:

> If to do were as easy as to know what were good to do, chapels had been churches, and poor men's cottages princes' palaces. It is a good divine that follows his own instructions: I can easier teach twenty what were good to be done, than be one of the twenty to follow mine own teaching.[21]

Not so with Christ! He "was a prophet, powerful in word and deed before God and all the people" (Luke 24:19). Many can teach truths. He *is* "the truth" (John 14:6).

Others may say, "Follow my teachings"; He calls, "Follow me" (Mark 1:17). Socrates inspired by courageous dying; Jesus conquered death (1 Cor. 15). While some people claim that all of Christ's teachings were already present in Judaism, Julius Wellhausen responded for Christians: "Yes, it is all in the Talmud—and how much else!"[22] For Christ not only fulfills and transcends the Old Testament but also simplifies and purifies the teachings and traditions which had almost hidden its message. Therefore, we may claim with Nicodemus, in a way more profoundly than he understood at the time, that Christ is, indeed, "a teacher who has come from God" (John 3:2).

The Resurrection

We all have many natural experiences which may prepare our hearts for the New Testament witness about Christ's resurrection. Very early, we confront the mystery of the origin of human life itself. If naturalists cannot explain the source of life and its continued personal existence, they should not be too critical of Christians who believe in the resurrection of Christ from the dead.

We continually exercise our wills and cause things to transpire in our bodies and the surrounding material world, so why should it seem unlikely that God could will the bodily resurrection of His Son? Fortunately we are not left on the threshold of these natural experiences, but we are given clear and tangible evidence for Christ's resurrection.

Not Done in a Corner

God began to prepare us for this miraculous event early in His redemptive dealings with the world. He delivered Israel from Egyptian bondage and enabled Miriam to sing with joy that they were delivered. God had not only revealed His Word spiritually but also "The horse and its rider he has hurled into the sea" (Ex. 15:21). God continued to break in upon the life of Israel, speaking through the prophets, preserving His children against all odds, and shaping a worship, a book, and a people. He was preparing them to believe in the triumph of His power and love over all evil.

Everything Christ said and did provided grounds for faith and hope that in Him every evil would be destroyed, even death. The disciples' early surprise and disbelief in the resurrection is difficult to understand because Christ Himself expected to rise and tried to prepare His disciples for the event. Mark wrote: "He then began to teach them that the Son of Man must suffer many things and be rejected by the elders, chief priests and teachers of the law, and that he must be killed and after three days rise again" (Mark 8:31). See also Mark 9:10 and Luke 18:31-33.

After Jesus had demonstrated against the moneychangers and those who were trafficking in the hopes and prayers of devout people, the authorities of the Temple asked Him, "What miraculous sign can you show us to prove your authority to do all this?" Jesus answered, "Destroy this temple, and I will raise it again in three days." This Christ said, speaking not of the actual Temple but of His body and resurrection. "After he was raised from the dead, his disciples recalled what He had said. Then they believed the Scripture true and the words that Jesus had spoken" (John 2:18-19, 22). Perhaps Christians will not be critical of the disciples' struggle to grasp the resurrection but will confess that, though believing in the resurrection, we often fail to live in the spirit of its victory.

A Candid Camera

The early followers of Jesus, far from creating the belief in the resurrection out of their own expectations, were actually surprised and bewildered by it. Although He had tried earnestly to prepare them for His resurrection, they were, like Martha at Lazarus's grave (John 11:24), still thinking of a general resurrection at the end of the world. With commendable honesty, the New Testament writers presented these disciples and early followers with candor. The very fact that they groped and fumbled to grasp the wonder of the resurrection of their Lord indicates they did not produce the idea out of their own spiritual enthusiasm and imagination.

The resurrection accounts could not be clearer in showing that human beings in their own strength were incapable of overcoming the disillusionment and defeat of Christ's crucifixion. The divine initiative dominates the narratives. The disciples in their own strength had failed, but God raised up Christ and many of the dead arose from their graves (Matt. 27:51-53). There simply was no expectation of a dying and rising Messiah.[23] And where did the disciples get the idea of a glorified body? The most convincing answer is that it could have come only from seeing the risen Lord in all His splendor.

Worth Dying For

All four Gospels make clear references to the empty tomb. This is tangible evidence for the resurrection. However, except for a rare occasion (John 20:8), the empty tomb alone did not produce the faith of the disciples. Faith came, rather, through their living encounter with Christ, as He called them to service and sacrifice. Christ is, therefore, no shallow projected guarantee for eternal life, but one who calls believers to give themselves, many in death, for His kingdom (see Matt. 28:19-20; Luke 24:47-49; Mark 16:15; John 20:22-23; 1 Cor. 9:1; Gal. 1:15-16).

Some of the first witnesses to the resurrection were faithful and persistent in their claims, even when confronted with suffering and death. This is worthy evidence that the resurrection was neither a hoax nor the result of some face-saving scheme on the part of the disciples. If the early followers had made up the stories, they had little to gain but outward persecution and a lifelong battle with guilt. It seems more reasonable to believe, rather, that hypocrites do not become good martyrs and that the resurrection happened.

This line of reasoning is, in fact, one of the first arguments used by the early church in defense of the resurrection. Eusebius, writing early in the fourth century, stressed that the disciples had nothing to gain by lying about the event. He pled ironically, almost humorously, when he rejected any suggestion that the disciples entered into a ridiculous plot to make up lies which could benefit no one involved. Their treachery could not aid themselves, those being deceived, or Christ Himself. What could be greater, they might have asked, than to give up everything just to deceive and be deceived?[24] A little later in the history of the church, Augustine used this same kind of logic to defend the Christian faith, asking: "Has anyone ever chosen death rather than deny, when commanded to deny, that Romulus and Hercules and the rest were gods?"[25]

Heralds of Spring

These traditional evidences may be needed by those of us who were not present for the event, but the resurrection burst in upon Christ's first followers like the beginning of the world. Reflecting upon Christ's gentle but compelling appearance to Mary Magdalene (John 20:11-18), G. K. Chesterton exclaimed: "What they were looking at was the first day of a new creation, with a new heaven and a new earth; and in a semblance of a gardener God walked again in the garden, in the cool not of the evening but the dawn."[26]

We too may experience this same risen Lord in our world. C. S. Lewis's words can help us claim this presence when he likened Christ's resurrection to the coming of spring:

To be sure, it feels wintry enough still: but often in the very early spring it feels like that. Two thousand years are only a day or two by this scale. A man really ought to say, "the Resurrection happened two thousand years ago" in the same spirit in which he says, "I saw a crocus yesterday." Because we know what is coming behind the crocus. The spring comes slowly down this way; but the great thing is that the corner has been turned.

Lewis went on to explain that in nature the crocus cannot choose to respond. But we have the choice, in Christ, either to reject Him and sink into eternal winter or to follow Him into new life and the glorious spring and summer where He already dwells.[27]

This message is in harmony with our deepest longings for life and hope. At the same time it is noble in moral and ethical goodness; it is unique in all the world, yet confirmed by abundant witnesses. It is spontaneous, joyful, and produces good works; it is extremely durable in times of testing and opposition. We believe such a gospel possesses all the characteristics of a divine revelation and redemption and points us to the Savior who is worthy of our total commitment.

Notes

1. John Bunyan, *The Pilgrim's Progress* (New York: Dutton, 1964), p. 13.

2. Bruce Metzger, *The Text of the New Testament* (New York and Oxford: Oxford University Press, 1968), p. 34.

3. Everett F. Harrison, *Introduction to the New Testament* (Grand Rapids: Eerdmans, 1964), p. 205.

4. Metzger, p. 86.

5. F. C. Grant, "The Greek Text of the New Testament," *An Introduction to the Revised Standard Version of the New Testament* (Chicago: International Council of Religious Education, 1946), p. 42

6. Herald Riesenfeld, "The Gospel Tradition and Its Beginnings," *The Gospel Tradition* (Philadelphia: Fortress, 1970), pp. 1-29.

7. See Joachim Jeremias, *New Testament Theology, The Proclamation of Jesus* (New York: Scribner's, 1971), pp. 29-37; J. A. T. Robinson, *Redating the New Testament* (Philadelphia: Westminster, 1976), pp. 354-358.

8. C. H. Dodd, *History of the Gospels* (New York: Scribner's, 1938), pp. 68-74.

9. F. F. Bruce, *The New Testament Documents: Are They Reliable?* (Grand Rapids: Eerdmans, 1960), p. 46.

10. Charles F. Pfeiffer, ed., *The Biblical World: A Dictionary of Biblical Archaeology* (Grand Rapids: Baker, 1966), pp. 457-458.

11. Jack Finegan, *The Archeology of the New Testament: The Life of Jesus and the Beginning of the Early Church* (Princeton: University Press, 1972), pp. 160-161.

12. Raymond E. Brown, *Recent Discoveries and the Biblical World* (Wilmington, Del.: Michael Glazier, Inc., 1983), p. 85.

13. Paul Tillich, *Systematic Theology* (Chicago: University of Chicago Press, 1951), I:27.

14. Barnabas Lindars, *New Testament Apologetic* (Philadelphia: Westminster, 1961), pp. 41, 46, 48-49.

15. W. Sanday, *Inspiration,* (New York: Longmans, Green, & Co., 1896), pp. 404-405.

16. A. B. Bruce, *Apologetics* (New York: Scribner's, 1904), p. 376.

17. Edward John Carnell, *The Kingdom of Love and the Pride of Life* (Grand Rapids: Eerdmans, 1960), p. 105.

18. A. M. Fairbairn, *The Philosophy of the Christian Religion* (New York: Macmillan, 1949), pp. 347-348.

19. Gerhard Ebeling, *Dogmatik des christlichen Glaubens, Der Glaube an Gott den Versoehner der Welt* (Tuebingen: J. C. B. Mohr [Paul Siebeck] 1979), Part 2, 2: 181; my translation.

20. Carl Ullmann, *The Sinlessness of Jesus: An Evidence for Christianity,* trans. Sophia Taylor from 7th German ed. (Edinburgh: T. & T. Clark, 1882), p. 64.

21. William Shakespeare, "The Merchant of Venice," in *The Complete Works of William Shakespeare* (Garden City, N.Y.: Garden City Publishing Co., 1936), Act I, Scene 2, lines 12-17, p. 449.

22. T. R. Glover, *The Christian Tradition and Its Verification* (London: Methuen, 1913), p. 203.

23. Sigmund Mowinckel, *He That Cometh,* trans. G. W. Anderson (Nashville: Abingdon, 1955), pp. 325-333.

24. Avery Dulles, *History of Apologetics* (New York: Corpus, 1971), p. 53.

25. Augustine, *The City of God,* trans. Gerald G. Walsh and D. J. Honan, *The Fathers of the Church,* vol. 24 (Washington: Catholic University of America Press, 1964), Book XXII, Ch. 6, p. 428.

26. G. K. Chesterton, *The Everlasting Man* (London: Hodder and Stoughton, 1947), p. 247.

27. C. S. Lewis, "The Grand Miracle," *God in the Dock* (Grand Rapids: Eerdmans, 1970), pp. 87-88.

8

I *Believe,* Therefore *I Am*

Long before the coming of Christ, Plato described our human predicament dramatically by portraying all of us as chained in a deep, dark cave. We had lived in the cave so long that we had become accustomed to the shadows and the dim flickering light from a fire burning behind us. We even made games for ourselves by seeking to identify the shadows cast on the wall by various objects, at times giving the shadows names of which we were very proud. Plato, however, longed earnestly for the time when the true teacher, the noble philosopher, would come loose our chains and lead us out to the sunlight of reality and truth.

The Old Testament, as we have seen, also recognized that we were in a state of spiritual darkness and bondage. Its writers longed for the coming of the Messiah who could set us free. Christians believe that these longings can be fulfilled in Christ. When He began His public ministry, Jesus returned to His hometown of Nazareth and was invited to speak at the synagogue. Calling for the scroll of the prophecy of Isaiah He read:

> The Spirit of the Lord is on me,
>> because he has anointed me
>> to preach good news to the poor.
> He has sent me to proclaim freedom for the prisoners
>> and recovery of sight for the blind,
> to release the oppressed,
>> to proclaim the year of the Lord's favor.

When He finished reading these words, all eyes were fastened on Him as He declared: "Today this scripture is fulfilled in your hearing" (Luke 4:18-19 [Isa. 61:1-2], 20-21).

Jesus comes to deliver all of us from whatever enslaves or prevents us from realizing our highest personal fulfillment. In Plato's story, the true sunlight of reality hurt the people's eyes, and many longed to return to the cave and the shadows. They even threatened to kill the philosopher. Similarly, many at Nazareth were offended at Jesus' liberating truth and desired to kill Him that very day (Luke 4:28-30). Even though He has come and is able to help us attain our potential, we have to be willing to receive His wholeness. We must still respond to His penetrating question to the paralyzed man, "Do you want to get well?" (John 5:6).

Be Yourself

To bring us this healing, Christ came into our twisted and perverted world at tremendous sacrifice. Boris Pasternak described this hostile world in his Nobel prize-winning novel, *Doctor Zhivago:*

> Rome was a flea market of borrowed Gods and conquered peoples; a bargain basement on two floors, earth and heaven; a mass of filth, convoluted in a triple knot . . . heavy wheels without spokes; eyes sunk in fat, sodomy, illiterate emperors; fish fed on the flesh of learned slaves. There were more people in the world than there have ever been since; all crammed in the passages of the coliseum and all wretched.

The novelist's prose almost takes the wings of poetry as he told of Christ's coming: "Into this tasteless heap of gold and marble He came; light and clothed in an aura. Emphatically human, deliberately provincial, Galilean; and at that moment Gods and nations ceased to be, and man came into being. . . ."[1] The Creator-Word became flesh so that He could make us into the persons we ought to *become.*

Before we romanticize what Christ wants us to become, we should look closely at Him and His followers who are our models for fulfillment. He had no place to lay His head, was often misunderstood, and eventually paid for His love and teachings with death on a cross. Paul fared little better than his Lord in matters of personal prestige, comforts, or material possessions. He was candid about his sufferings, yet triumphant about his joy and fulfillment when he declared that as servants of God we commend ourselves

> through glory and dishonor, bad report and good report: genuine, yet regarded as imposters; known, yet regarded as unknown; dying, and yet

we live on; beaten, and yet not killed; sorrowful, yet always rejoicing; poor, yet making many rich; having nothing, and yet possessing everything (2 Cor. 6:8-10).

This call for surrender should not surprise us, for from the beginning of the journey, Christ challenges us to take up our cross and follow Him.

Reach for the Stars

What kind of beings we are, anyway, who continually, and at times frantically, seek personal fulfillment? What does it mean to be a person? Why can't we just be content to exist, to survive our relatively short time of life without these restless dreams? The answer lies in the fact that we are not just sense modules limited to our present time and space, but are transcendent beings. We are created to live responsibly in this—and another—world. Sociologist Peter Berger in his highly respected book, *A Rumor of Angels,* described "five signals for transcendence" in human personality:

1. Our propensity for *order,* which causes us to want to soothe a child by saying everything is all right even though it is not, thus pointing toward an *ultimate* order that is not yet realized.

2. Our delight in joyful *play* activity, which makes times stand still, pointing toward *eternity.*

3. The presence of a death-defying *courage* and hope, even in the face of death, promising *immortality.*

4. A *moral* revulsion to monstrous evil wherein events like the Holocaust cry out not only for a heaven but also a hell.

5. The transcendent character of *humor* even in the midst of impossible situations, implying the existence of *another* world.[2]

While space will not allow each of these signals to be treated fully, the overall impression may provide a witness to our personal transcendence. Our very restlessness should confirm that we are made for, and called to, a better world.

Free Indeed

The Bible teaches that Adam and Eve sinned and were cast out of the garden (Gen. 3). We, like them, have sinned (Rom. 5:12; 3:23). When this sin is not forgiven, people live in misery. Personal fulfillment can come only when we are released from this burden of guilt. Many people in our modern world do not expect to stand before a great heavenly throne with their sins recorded in a large book. However, they are anxious and aware of not having realized their full human potential. Here the Christian message strives to make contact with their inner feelings and to explain that they have sinned against their Creator, and their guilt is real, and they are in need of forgiveness.

Until forgiveness comes, we all struggle like John Bunyan's pilgrim, weighted down with a tremendous burden of guilt. All our efforts to get rid of it seem only to make it heavier and more grievous to bear. We may find release, however, if we, like Christian, come to the hill called Calvary, bow beneath the cross of Christ, and surrender our lives to Him. Now the burden bolts from Christian's back and rolls down the hill into the mouth of the empty tomb of the risen Lord. We can almost hear Bunyan shout, *"and [he] saw it no more!"*[3] Leslie Weatherhead called this forgiveness "the most powerful therapeutic idea in the world."[4]

Christians experience liberation and joy in being free from the cares of the world because we no longer belong to the world. God's love frees us from the entanglements which have held us for so long and marred even our best days with a stain of bitterness. What a glorious relief to be truly delivered from our past and liberated from its oppressive presence! Trapped in an unendurable situation, we are set free by the word of forgiveness.

> We have escaped like a bird
> out of the fowler's snare;
> the snare has been broken
> and we have escaped (Ps. 124:7).

The Strong Man's House

The New Testament also teaches that forgiveness is more than merely changing our attitude or ideas about human morality, or right and wrong. Only through Christ's victory over the *supernatural* powers of evil is forgiveness possible. He has dealt with the problem of sin at the very citadel of Satan. Christ has bound Satan in order to assure our deliverance (Mark 3:27).

In fact, God has turned our defeat and death in sin into a spiritual parade of triumph greater than the Roman's celebrations of victory over their enemies. He allows those who were dead in sins to be made alive together with Christ:

> He forgave us all our sins, having canceled the written code, with its regulations, that was against us and that stood opposed to us; he took it away, nailing it to the cross. And having disarmed the powers and authorities, he made a public spectacle of them, triumphing over them by the cross (Col. 2:13-15).

What could be more liberating and personally fulfilling than to experience a release from the haunting agony of knowing we were not right with ourselves, the world, or God!

God's forgiveness is, however, not merely a legal declaration which leaves us spiritually and morally unchanged. Rather, the love of Christ comes so graciously to us that we are drawn away from our sin and motivated to become more like Him.

In Rome during the days when Flavius Honorius was emperor, thousands used to gather in a huge amphitheater to watch the cruel gladiatorial combats. A sensitive Christian named Telemachus traveled more than a thousand miles from Asia Minor to Rome in order to stop this inhuman spectacle. He was unsuccessful in many attempts to accomplish his purpose. Finally one day he ran into the arena and begged the gladiators to stop killing one another. Shocked and enraged by such a presumptuous interference with their pleasure, the spectators poured down upon the field and killed Telemachus.

This sacrificial intervention brought many to their senses and eventually led the emperor to forbid the gladiatorial slaughter. What if we had been prisoners in a Roman cell, expecting any moment to be called into the arena and forced to kill or be killed? But then the news comes. We are allowed to go free because Telemachus, a good man, died. Imagine our rejoicing and lifelong gratitude as we return to life, home, and the freedom to pursue our dreams. Christ on the cross did this and much more!

We may still, on occasion, sin. But we are to endeavor in repentance and faith to remain close to God's Word and the fellowship of His people. We can claim with John that God through "the blood of Jesus, his Son, purifies us from every sin" (1 John 1:7). This verse means that

Christ *keeps on cleansing us.* We need this continual grace from God so desperately that even if science could demonstrate effectively the immortality of the soul, we would still, without forgiveness, be personally incomplete and unfulfilled.

Finding Our Balance

Many who have never known or have lost contact with the ultimate spiritual values of life live in profound loneliness, dread, and relentless fear. This wretched state of existence is, according to Paul Tillich, the anxiety which comes from experiencing a loss of meaning in life:

> The anxiety of meaninglessness is anxiety about the loss of an ultimate concern, of a meaning which gives meaning to all meanings. This anxiety is aroused by a loss of a spiritual center, of an answer, however symbolic and indirect, to the question to the meaning of existence.[5]

This happens when people give their ultimate loyalties to secondary objects or projects, such as their nation, sex, sport, wealth, power, or even to beloved persons. None of these is worthy of ultimate allegiance. Often one flits from one object of loyalty to another only to experience the cooling of the emotions and to lapse into indifference or aversion. "Everything is tried and nothing satisfies."[6]

Our need for an object of loyalty worthy of our ultimate commitment was acknowledged by psychologist Wayne Oates when he perceived:

> The integration of personality rests largely upon the integrity, durability, and eternal nature of the object of loyalty around which personality is integrated. When the central meaning, the main object of loyalty, is never discovered or proves to be false, perishes by death or for any reason collapses, the person must either discover a new center, a new loyalty, or perish himself of sheer meaninglessness.[7]

In other words, for us to be fulfilled as human beings, we need intellect, will, and emotion to work together toward that which is ultimate and eternal. We need that loyalty which Josiah Royce called, "the will to believe in something eternal and to express that belief in the practical life of a human being."[8]

Jesus Christ is eternally durable and comprehensively relevant to every phase of our lives. He is ready to give daily guidance and strength. He can help us thread a needle, plant a crop, or rocket to the moon.

My beloved teacher, Emile Cailliet of Princeton, enjoyed telling the following story to show the practical results of being a Christian. A young American student was having trouble finding himself and went to Dr. James Martineau for counsel. The student was full of zeal for the eradication of all religion. The minister advised him to spend six months with a simple Westphalian Christian peasant family and six months among cultured and emancipated German students. After those experiences, the student was to ask himself which were wiser and more fulfilled.

When the student returned, he confessed that the peasant family seemed better able to deal with the grim realities of life. They possessed a depth of insight, an assurance of action, and at-homeness of conviction that was swift, pure, and massive. When the nimble, enlightened, and materialistic students were faced with grim realities, they were utterly helpless, without insight, action, or conviction of any kind. This is the truth of the testimonies of the New Testament believers. They were not foolishly thankful *for* everything that happened but had the grace and strength to "give thanks *in* all circumstances" (1 Thess. 5:18, author's italics).

Putting It All Together

Our psychological growth and personal fulfillment are partly shaped by the worth of that to which we give our ultimate loyalty. The value of our personal role models and the intensity of our allegiance to them also influences our growth and fulfillment. How well we integrate these influences into the interests and activities of our lives is another factor.[9] We tend to become like our heroes. How wonderful, then, to give our loyalty, in fact, our worship, to Christ the God-man. He became truly human, not just some vague abstract humanity but a particular little baby who grew into the man Jesus of Nazareth. We, therefore, worship Him and call Him Lord, in part because He perfectly embodies what we are to follow, indeed, what we as His children want to become. To follow Jesus means to be "humanized" by Him and to realize the highest reaches of our human worth.

Not only is Christ our example of what it means to be a full person but also His teaching imparts God's deepest wisdom for effective living. Concerning this teaching, psychiatrist James T. Fisher has given this tribute:

> If you were to take the sum total of all the authoritative articles ever written by the most qualified of psychologists and psychiatrists on the subject of mental hygiene—if you were to combine them and refine them and cleave out the excess verbiage—if you were to take the whole of the meat and none of the parsley, and if you were to have these unadulterated bits of pure scientific knowledge concisely expressed by the most capable of living poets, you would have an awkward and incomplete summation of the Sermon on the Mount.[10]

In a profound psychological sense, then, we may claim with Paul that Christ "is our peace" (Eph. 2:14). He is our peace in that He gives us forgiveness to remove our guilt; He gives us courage instead of fear; we receive the confidence of love to replace our self-centeredness; He offers us companionship in the midst of loneliness; He is an indwelling strength and presence when we are powerless; and we have hope now and in the future to overcome our despair. This is truly personal fulfillment!

Stooping to Conquer

Our fulfillment through Christ is possible only because He endured suffering and overcame the world. It was, as the writer of Hebrews explained, clearly fitting "that God, for whom and through whom everything exists, should make the author of their salvation perfect through suffering" (Heb. 2:10). As difficult as it may be to accept, God allows pain and suffering (which, as we have said, only entered the world as a result of sin) to point us beyond this world to our need for Him.

The suffering of this world can only make sense if we allow it to point us beyond the pain to One who is calling us to a better time and place. We are like those migratory birds in the North who feel the chill of the approach of winter and instinctively, with a pain we can only imagine, must wing their way to a warmer refuge. The more seriously we take the problem of suffering the more clearly it gives witness to the reality of greater values which may be realized. If suffering did not point us beyond itself to God, it would present no mystery; it would only "exist." The washing away of the stones on the shore merely "takes place." The wasting away of our physical bodies through disease and age, however, is a problem of tragic proportion. But it is a problem only to the degree that bodily health and life itself are deemed *valuable*. Perhaps, then, we can understand the problem of suffering as an evidence *for* the existence of values which can only be sustained by belief in a personal God and a risen Christ.

The Two Messengers

Some have lived through deep waters and fiery trials and give glorious testimony to God's faithfullness and their consciousness of personal fulfillment in times of sorrow and suffering. Simone Weil wrote triumphantly out of poverty, hunger, and an injured body scarcely ever free of pain:

> Joy and suffering are two equally precious gifts both of which must be savored to the full, each one in its purity, without trying to mix them. Through joy, the beauty of the world penetrates our soul. Through suffering it penetrates our body. We could no more become friends of God through joy alone than one becomes a ship's captain by studying books on navigation. The body plays a part in all apprenticeships. On the plane of physical sensibility, suffering alone gives us contact with that necessity which constitutes the order of the world. . . . the transforming power of suffering and of joy are equally indispensable. When either of them comes to us we have to open the very center of our soul to it, just as a woman opens her door to messengers from her beloved one. What does it matter to a lover if the messenger be polite or rough, so long as he delivers the message?[11]

Paul experienced this in his prayerful striving to be rid of his thorn in the flesh. In spite of his suffering he learned to bear it joyfully and proclaim with unshakable conviction that Christ's grace is sufficient and His "power is made perfect in weakness" (2 Cor. 12:9).

In the light of such testimonies, we may understand that personal fulfillment is not a natural category derived from human experience that we may use to test the truth of the Christian faith. Rather, Christian experience itself has become our standard and norm for the kind of personal fulfillment which cannot be surpassed. Christ alive makes His presence and purposes known to us, even as He did to the disciples on the road to Emmaus. If our hearts are broken and our plans shattered, He can make our hearts burn within us while He walks and talks with us on our way (Luke 24:13-35). All our questions may not be answered but He makes *Himself* known and that, for the one who believes, is more than enough.

We Are Family

Christ also has a way of bringing us fulfillment in our relations with one another. As Cailliet said,

> Christian friendship is an election. We Christians need not cultivate the techniques of "how to make friends and influence people." We identify our new friends as the Lord sends them along the appointed way. In this connection also we are the people of the Way.[12]

The Christian life not only enhances our esteem and delight in our friends but also provides the desire and strength to follow Christ's example and teaching to love our enemies.

We must acknowledge that *two* persons who are willing to live in harmony are necessary for a peaceful relationship. However, it is possible to be so secure in Christ's love that we can allow Him, through us, to love our enemies. This cannot be achieved by moral striving but only through the miracle of Christ's grace and presence.

Corrie ten Boom demonstrated the power of this gift when, after speaking in a Christian service in Germany, she encountered her former cruel Nazi prison guard. The guard's malicious torture swam vividly before her eyes as he approached her to speak after her message. She feared she could not face him. Even after he told her he had become a Christian, she did not feel she could forgive him. However, she prayed honestly to the Lord and even confessed she felt no love in her heart. Silently she told God she would by strength of will raise her arm to shake the man's hand and trust Christ to provide the grace. Then, she wrote, "as I took his hand the most incredible thing happened. From my shoulder along my arm and through my hand a current seemed to pass from me to him, while into my heart sprang a love for this stranger that almost overwhelmed me."[13]

By following Christ we may become truly human, the very persons we were intended to be. Anthony Campolo once asked a group of students what they wanted out of life. One answered, "I want to become human—fully human." To this earnest longing the teacher replied after further discussion, "Doesn't Jesus possess the fullness of humanity? Isn't He infinitely loving, graciously forgiving, totally emphathetic, and infinitely aware of people in the world in which He lives?"[14] Because Paul believed that "in Christ all the fullness of the Deity lives in bodily form," he could add for the believer, "and you have been given fullness in Christ" (Col. 2:9-10).

The Tree of Life

Our personal fulfillment will not be, nor was it ever intended to be, completely realized in this life. We will continue to struggle here and, on occasion no doubt, experience pain and bitter defeat. But this is not the last word! God promises even in the Old Testament that one who follows Him "is like a tree planted by streams of water, which yields its fruit in season and whose leaf does not wither" (Ps. 1:3).

And in the New Testament the tree of Calvary is aglow with eternal goodness and renewed life. Paul assured the Christian that Christ "himself bore our sins in his body on the tree, so that we might die to sins and live for righteousness; by his wounds you have been healed" (1 Pet. 2:24). Furthermore, God promises that in heaven there is the tree of life, unlike our trees, "bearing twelve crops of fruit, yielding its fruit every month. And the leaves of the tree are for the healing of the nations" (Rev. 22:2). Here and now we are often painfully aware of limitations and disappointments, "but all the leaves of the New Testament are rustling with the rumor that it will not always be so."[15]

Beyond Imagination

In heaven we shall experience a fulfillment where even our wishes are inspired perfectly by the holy and powerful love of our Creator. The agonizing distance between our desires and that which our wills are able to accomplish will no longer exist. Is not this the "crown of righteousness" which Paul expected to receive (2 Tim. 4:8)? Life will no longer be stained and weakened by sin, but we will always be doing that which is *right!* No wonder "the whole creation is on tiptoe to see the wonderful sight of the sons of God coming into their own" (Rom. 8:19, Phillips).

Anyone who receives Christ's grace will experience this fulfillment. We will not have to wait for aeons, nor will we be alone. But life will be continually creative and our joy beautiful and complete. I like to believe that after arriving on that far shore we will behold our Lord in all His glory and draw near to those we love as His redeemed. Then we will look around at our new world and fellowship and exclaim that our fulfillment is all immeasurably more than we could have asked or imagined (Eph. 3:20).

Notes

1. Boris Pasternak, *Doctor Zhivago*, trans. Max Hayward and Manya Hareari (New York: Pantheon Books, Inc., 1958), p. 43.

2. Peter Berger, *A Rumor of Angels* (Garden City, N. Y.: Doubleday, 1969), pp.65-90.

3. John Bunyan, *The Pilgrim's Progress* (New York: Dutton, 1964), p. 39.

4. Leslie Weatherhead, *Psychology, Religion and Healing* (Nashville: Abingdon, 1951), p. 338.

5. Paul Tillich, *The Courage to Be* (New Haven: Yale University Press, 1952), p. 47.

6. Ibid., p. 48.

7. Wayne Oates, *What Psychology Says About Religion* (New York: Association Press, 1958), p. 94.

8. Josiah Royce, *The Philosophy of Loyalty* (New York: Macmillan, 1920), p. 357.

9. Henry N. and Regina W. Wieman, "Appraising Religious Growth," *Readings in Psychology of Religion*, ed. Orlo Strunk, Jr. (Nashville: Abingdon, 1959), pp. 165-172.

10. James T. Fisher and Lowell S. Hawley, *A Few Buttons Missing, The Case Book of a Psychiatrist* (Philadelphia: Lippincott, 1951), p. 273.

11. Simone Weil, *Waiting for God*, trans. Emma Craufurd (New York: Capricorn Books), p. 132.

12. Emile Cailliet, *Journey Into Light* (Grand Rapids: Zondervan, 1968), p. 21.

13. Corrie ten Boom, *The Hiding Place* (Washington Depot, Conn.: Chosen Books, 1971), p. 215.

14. Anthony Campolo, *A Reasonable Faith: Responding to Secularism* (Waco, Tex.: Word Books, 1983), p. 161.

15. C. S. Lewis, *The Weight of Glory* (New York: Macmillan, 1949), p. 13.

9

Morning Has Broken

While the personal fulfillment that Christ brings to a believer is an internal evidence for the truth of the Christian faith, much positive external evidence for the faith can be seen in history. Christ came not only to make us individually whole, but to unite us with Him and with one another in a community of belief which He calls the church. It is His body. Just as He came from eternity into time, so the church is called to give its testimony for Him at the crossroads of history.

Earthen Vessels

Christians must sorrowfully confess that through the centuries sins and crimes have been committed in association with the name of Christ and His church. Even if we clearly distinguish between the *true* church of Christ—a fellowship of those joined together under His lordship—and the mere institutional organization operating under His name, we still cannot completely separate ourselves from the sins of the church. We may identify with the humble spirit of Visser't Hooft, an active, witnessing Christian who requested ordination so he would "be more closely identified with the wretchedness of the church."[1]

Guilty of Sin

Segments of Christ's church have been guilty of grievous sins at times. Christians have been arrogantly greedy, selfish, and consumed with power. The church has been cowardly reticent to act against slavery and other inhumanities. The Inquisition and the abuses of the Crusades are part of church history. The church has frequently opposed scientific progress, as in the cases of Bacon, Galileo, and Bruno. The church has shown an embarrassing reluctance to speak and act

125

courageously for political and economic freedom and human rights. If we wish to disassociate ourselves from these failures, we can do so only if we confess many of these same attitudes and patterns in our own lives and churches and ask forgiveness as we earnestly try to do better.

We can also plead with our critics to evaluate the church as charitably as they do other social and cultural institutions. For example, does anyone deny the early contributions of Greek philosophy, art, medicine, or politics because some city-state councilmen in Athens were responsible for the death of Socrates? The Christian church, on the whole, is probably more repentant of its mistakes and failures than other institutions. Did the ancient Roman empire repent of its cruelties and atrocities in conquest; the Barbarians of their inhuman subjection of many races; the Eastern religions of the injustices of caste; and Marxism of its strangling of freedom and life in its many purges? But many in the church have often acknowledged failures. We confess that the treasure of the gospel of Christ is, indeed, carried "in jars of clay" (2 Cor. 4:7).

Just Beginning

Christ realized that the influence of the gospel through the church would be gradual, at times almost imperceptible. He knew His kingdom would come like yeast working through slowly rising dough, as a grain of mustard seed which can hardly be seen, or even as the seed which grows secretly and mysteriously in the night while the world sleeps. He chose to work patiently through personality and human freedom, recognizing that it takes time for a disciple to mature and for a rebellious race to receive and reflect the kingdom of God on earth.

Any evaluation of the church and its influence in the world needs a wide and charitable perspective on historical time. Imagine taking the book you hold to the top of the Empire State Building in New York City. Lay the book flat on the topmost ledge and try to imagine that the distance from the ground to the ledge represents the time since *human* history began. The relatively small width of the book resting on the ledge could represent the brief time of *church* history. Think now of the centuries of personal and institutional wrongs which have needed reshaping. If this perspective be granted, we may be amazed at the impact of the gospel upon history!

The Miracle of the Church

The very establishment and survival of the church is a miracle. When Christ inaugurated His church at Caesarea Philippi following Simon Peter's confession of Him as the Son of the living God, the church was surrounded by seemingly insurmountable difficulties. The tremendous crowds which had followed Christ in the great Galilean ministry had already stopped following Him because He refused to be a political messiah. Disunity and conflict stirred among the apostles themselves. Even Simon Peter only partially understood his Lord's words about the cross. Nevertheless, Christ was confident that those whom He had "called out" would grow in understanding and commitment and that the church would survive, for it was founded upon a rock (Matt. 16:13-20; Rom. 9:33; 1 Cor. 10:4).

Only through a miracle of grace could the church have survived. The early church did not have the institutional support of Israel, the military might of Rome, the learning of the Greeks or any other early civilization. It certainly had no wealth. Nor, to be perfectly honest, did it have any commanding personal presence or magnetism among the early disciples.

Once Frederick the Great of Germany demanded that his prime minister give him one good reason for believing in God. The prime minister, recalling the survival of the Hebrew people, responded without hesitation, "The Jews, your Majesty!" The Christian, recalling the survival of the church can respond, "The church! One evidence for believing in our Lord is the survival of His church!"

Staying Power

From the beginning, the church swam upstream against pagan immorality in the Greco-Roman world. It dared to proclaim that its Leader, a despised outcast who had been crucified, had risen from the dead and is yet alive! Could any message be more audacious or any hope less likely to endure? But this Christian community not only survived but also thrived! It transcended a sterile but powerful Jewish legalism; mystery religions, such as Mithraism; the church's most likely moral contender, Manichaenism; the intellectual snobbery of

Gnosticism; the noblest expressions of Stoicism; and even the ingratiating emperor-deity cults.

The church has outlived the civilizations of antiquity, the feudalistic Dark Ages, the stagnant Middle Ages, the frantic Renaissance, the cold Age of Reason, the violent Age of Revolution, and continues alive and well in today's Age of Science and Technology. G. K. Chesterton paid tribute to these durable qualities of the church when he declared:

> If our social relations and records retain their continuity, if men really learn to apply reason to the accumulating facts of so crushing a story, it would seem that sooner or later even its enemies will learn from their incessant and interminable disappointments not to look for anything so simple as its death. They may continue to war with it, but it will be as they war with nature; as they war with the landscape, as they war with the skies. . . . They will watch for it to stumble; they will watch for it to err; they will no longer watch for it to end.[2]

The Preservers of the World

The mere survival of a fellowship or an institution, regardless of how unlikely this may have been, does not prove its worth; nor does this alone prove its divine origin. But the church not only survives but also does so creatively and benevolently, lifting and enriching those who come in contact with its loving spirit.

This was true during New Testament times and from the earliest days when the church loosed its Palestinian mooring and began sailing in the crosscurrents of surrounding cultures. Clement wrote in his Epistle to the Corinthians of the everwidening and elevating influence of early Christians as they began to permeate the Mediterranean world: "A profound and abundant peace was given to you all, and you had an insatiable desire for doing good, while a full outpouring of the Holy Spirit was upon you all."[3]

An unknown author of the Epistle to Diognetus wrote that the early Christians were not distinguished from other people by locality, speech, or customs. Rather, he said:

> They dwell in their own countries, but simply as sojourners. As citizens, they share in all things with others, and yet endure all things as if foreigners. Every foreign land is to them as their native country, and

every land of their birth as a land of strangers. . . . They pass their days on earth, but they are citizens of heaven.

The epistle explains that these Christians endured severe persecution, yet they were to the world what the soul is to the body. "Christians are confined in the world as in a prison, yet they are preservers of the world."[4]

Witnesses Unaware

In the early centuries, even the enemies of the church sometimes gave unintentional tributes to its spirit and practices. For example, Celsus, perhaps the most learned and fierce opponent of the church in its early decades, wrote condescendingly that other religious groups call for those who are holy and pure, "everyone who has clean hands and a prudent tongue. But let us hear what kind of persons these Christians invite." He called the roll with a sneer: sinners, housebreakers, thieves, burglars, prisoners, robbers of temple and tomb. To this scathing criticism, Origen responded that such a welcome by the church to sinners and outcasts is in itself a sign of its divine character.[5]

Another unconscious tribute to the benevolent influence of Christianity upon society may be seen in the fourth century when Julian, the apostate emperor, sought to imitate the Christian charities. After the Roman persecutions had failed to destroy the church, Julian sought in vain to revive Hellenistic paganism by infusing it with some of the Christian virtues. He wrote to the high priest of Galatia:

> The Hellenic religion does not yet prosper as I desire, and it is the fault of those who profess it. . . . In every city establish frequent hostels in order that strangers may profit by our benevolence; I do not mean for our own people only, but for others also who are in need of money. . . . For it is disgraceful that, when no Jew ever has to beg, and the impious Galileans [Christians] support not only their own poor but ours as well, all men see that our people lack aid from us. . . . Then let us not, by allowing others to outdo us in good works . . . utterly abandon the reverence due to the gods.[6]

That kind of borrowing or imitation of Christian values did not cease with Julian. It happens whenever any religious or secular movement needs the support of the *highest* virtues.

The Rising Sun

Although most testimonies for the benevolent character and work of the early church admittedly come from Christian sources, they are widespread and of such noble character as to be taken seriously. Tertullian, for example, wrote how Christians fed and buried the poor, cared for orphans, slaves, and ship-wrecked sailors, while pagans poked fun at simpleminded Christians whose benevolence could so easily be cheated.

Early Social Service

The *Didascalia,* an early treatise describing the life and organization of the church in Syria in the third century, gives instructions on caring for orphans. The pastors were to help them become adopted, arrange marriages where possible for the girls, teach the boys a trade, and help them all to become self-reliant.

In the late third century when plague broke out in Africa after fierce persecution by the emperor Decius, there was a general flight and panic, but many Christians remained to care for the sick and bury the dead. This same pattern occurred in Egypt after the devastating persecution under Valerian. And those familiar with the benevolence of the early church in the Book of Acts will not be surprised to learn that the church at Rome in the middle of the third century was sustaining 1,500 widows and poor; a few decades later the church at Antioch was caring for 3,000; and Constantinople had 7,000 on its maintenance rolls. Again, while our sources are admittedly Christian, it appears that paganism did not measure up to Christianity in the realm of social service.[7]

By the Sign of the Cross—Conquer

There can be little doubt that Constantine's Edict of Milan in AD 313 owed its inspiration to Christian influence and contributed greatly to social welfare and progress. Constantine's legislation attacked the old Roman custom of exposing unwanted infants, aided children of the poor by officially approving gifts for needy families, and strengthened the legal protection of minors. The liberation of slaves became easier, and breaking up slave families was forbidden. Branding slaves on the face was no longer allowed because the face was "fashioned after the likeness of the heavenly beauty." Prison conditions and penal practices improved. Efforts were made to raise the standard of sexual morality and strengthen the stability of the home throughout the empire.[8]

These improvements, which were influenced by the church, seem small alongside Christ's example and teachings; however, compared with the moral depravity of the times and the distance to be traveled toward the goal, they were monumental. Such moral progress allowed historian W. E. H. Lecky to conclude:

> The high conception that has been formed of the sanctity of human life, the protection of infancy, the elevation and final emancipation of the slave classes, the suppression of the barbarous games, the creation of the vast and multifarious organisation of charity, and the education of the imagination by the Christian type, constitute together a movement of philanthropy which has never been paralleled or approached in the Pagan world.[9]

Lecky retained this conviction and more than two decades later declared that the Christian religion had probably done more "to quicken the affections of mankind, to promote pity, to create a pure and merciful ideal, than any other influence that has ever acted on the world."[10]

Although the church has assuredly been instrumental in elevating the moral and social quality of life, documenting this creative, permeating power is like trying to evaluate the life-giving qualities of the sun. Seasons can be charted, temperatures recorded, harvests weighed, but who would dare estimate the value of light for the existence and enrichment of life? It is, however, possible to identify a few spiritual rays to illustrate the Christian influence for good in human history.

The prophet spoke for God, declaring, "For you who revere my name, the sun of righteousness will rise with healing in its wings" (Mal. 4:2). Some facets of the healing progress which reflect this sun of righteousness, Christ the Light of the world, deserve consideration.

Save the Children

At the very time when Jesus was born, the practice of abandoning newborn children to the natural elements or the arbitrary mercy of those passing by was widespread in the Roman world. A Roman soldier named Hilarion wrote his wife on June 17, 1 BC, encouraging the exposure and inevitable death of a baby girl. The ancient author Quintilian regarded the abandonment of infants as a beautiful custom. But Christ encouraged the little children to come to Him (Mark 10:14). Early church leaders like Clement, Origen, and Tertullian courageously attacked infanticide. Since those days, Christians have been instrumental in raising the standards for child worth and care throughout the world.

In our own century in the slums of Shinkawa in Kobe, Japan, a mild-mannered sensitive Christian with the courage of a giant determined to take Christ's model of service and sacrifice literally. Toyohiko Kagawa moved into a hovel surrounded by millions of industrial workers and their families who barely survived in subhuman conditions. Kagawa shared his earnings with them, endured their abuse, refusing to fight back, and carried scars from their cruelty the rest of his life. When a tiny feverish, near-starving baby girl was left at his door, he cared for her through the days and nights as tenderly as a single man could. In his poem, "When Tears Are Mingled," he wrote poignantly of his little Ishi's struggle for life:

> Dawn coming in through the greyness
> Lights up the place where she lies;
> I am sodden with sleep, but I waken
> At my starveling's fretful cries.
> She is here on the floor beside me
>   Wrapped in rags that stink;
> I change them; I hold her to feed her,
> And sob as she struggles to drink.
>
> ....
>
>   Cry again, little Ishi;
>   Cry once more, once more;
> What will it take to make you wake?
>   For I cannot let you go!
> I call; but you do not hear me;
> I clasp you; you do not move.
> It is not to pain I would bring you again,
> There is Love in the world; there is Love!
>   Will she not cry?
>   I shall make her;

Here in my close embrace
I kiss her wan lips growing greyer;
My drawn face touches her face.
Fast are my frightened tears flowing,
Falling on Ishi's eyes;
With her cold, still tears they are mingled.
O God . . . at last . . . she cries![11]

Eternity alone can reveal the effects of this kind of Christian love where compassion becomes incarnate in social action.

Let My People Go

Although today we may feel that the gospel's liberating influence on the practice and institution of slavery was inexcusably slow, we should remember the lack of social status and power of the early church. Jesus was a crucified outcast and Christians were a tiny band of close-knit followers just beginning to explore the social implications of their new faith. It might have been suicidal, or at least utterly hopeless, for those first believers to attack the institution of slavery directly.

At least they tried to improve the conditions of slaves and to instill the conviction of the inherent worth of all, whether "bond or free" (Gal. 3:28; Col. 3:11). The stance of the early church on this issue compares quite favorably with the social consciousness of other contemporary alternatives, such as Platonism, Stoicism, and the mystery religions. Let us also be careful lest we criticize the sins of these early Christians and overlook our need for clear vision and courageous action against the more subtle forms of "slavery" in our own day.

Unfortunately, some complex theological convictions held by Augustine and other leading Christian interpreters delayed the church's progress in this area. Some maintained with the Stoics that all persons are internally free by the law of nature but thought that repressive social conditions were condoned by God as a result of the fall. Many have believed that servitude by some races was ordained by God as a result of the curse placed on the descendents of Ham in the covenant made with Noah. Even so, the Lateran Council of 1179 decreed that all Christians should be free. This was progress, but there was much more to come.

Surely many factors were involved in the eventual abolition of slavery. But in those societies which came under Christian influence, a spiritual recognition of the dignity and worth of every human being helped to bring slaves their freedom. The following stories illustrate and symbolize the church's contribution to this liberation.

In God's Image

One day in Central Africa in 1861 David Livingstone, accompanied by an exploring party of the Universities' Mission, boldly wrenched slave sticks from the necks of a captive gang of slaves. This dramatic event characterized Livingstone's heroic struggle against slavery until his death—and his influence beyond. His biographer wrote:

> From the worn-out figure kneeling at the bedside in the hut in Ilala an electric spark seemed to fly, quickening hearts on every side. The statesmen felt it; it put new vigor into the dispatches he wrote and the measures he devised with regard to the slave-trade. The merchant felt it, and began to plan in earnest how to traverse the continent with roads and railways, and open it to commerce from shore to centre. The explorer felt it, and started with high purpose on new scenes of unknown danger. The missionary felt it,—felt it a reproof of past langour and unbelief, and found himself lifted up to a higher level of faith and devotion. No parliament of philanthropy was held; but the verdict was as unanimous and as hearty as if the Christian world had met and passed the resolution—"Livingstone's work shall not die; Africa Shall Live."[12]

Called By God's Name

When Harriet Beecher Stowe published an unassuming novel called *Uncle Tom's Cabin* in 1852, she fearlessly unmasked the institution of slavery in America. She revealed its greed, cruelty, and the profound immorality of both the slaveholder and those who sat complacently back and did nothing about the injustice. In one memorable scene the slaveholder, Simon Legree, is taking possession of his new property, Uncle Tom. Legree callously discards several of Uncle Tom's cheap but sentimental treasures and discovers Tom's hymn-book:

> "Humpf! Pious, to be sure. So, what's yer name,—you belong to the church, eh?"
> "Yes, Mas'r," said Tom, firmly.

"Well, I'll soon have *that* out of you. I have none o'yer bawling, praying, singing niggers on my place; so remember. Now, mind yourself," he said, with a stamp and a fierce glance of his gray eye, directed at Tom. *"I'm your church now!* You understand—you've got to be as *I say."*

Something within the silent black man answered *No!* and, as if repeated by an invisible voice came the words of an old prophetic scroll, as Eva had often read them to him,—"Fear not! for I have redeemed thee. I have called thee by my name. Thou art mine!"[13]

Christ, who was Himself executed like a slave for our liberation, has risen and calls us by name for freedom.

The Spirit of the Law

There is clear evidence that Christian teaching regarding the value of the individual is largely responsible for the elevation of human rights in law. While Christian attitudes have been a leavening influence wherever they have touched the legal systems of the world, the most tangible evidence of the gospel's impact on the development of law is in the church's canon law. T. Plucknett wrote of this influence on Europe in the twelfth century:

> At every opportunity the Church freed the law of contract from formalism, and finally declared, in spite of the Roman Maxim no legal action arises from a bare agreement, that a simple promise was enforceable. It must have needed a great deal of courage to reach this position when against it was all the authority of Roman law and the custom and practice of most of the other systems of secular law.[14]

This religious use of "good faith" in the legal realm was destined to make its contribution also in the field of economics in such areas as banking, insurance, and capital investments.

These beginnings also contributed to the development of international law. Hugo Grotius, a Dutch Christian theologian, first systematized the principles of international law in a book entitled *Right of War and Peace*. Grotius's proposals were based on both nature and the Christian faith. He challenged the right of nations to make slaves (which had been granted in the Roman *Law of Nations*), pleaded for the use of arbitration in the settling of international disputes, and proposed an international court.

The Rock from Which You Were Cut

Christian principles also undergirded English law which owes its origin, or at least its definitive shape, to the laws of Alfred the Great. Alfred's legal patterns, though Germanic with some original humanitarian clauses, are deliberately set within a biblical context and prefaced by multiple texts from the Bible, including the Ten Commandments, portions of the Mosaic law, excerpts from the Sermon on the Mount, and the Book of Acts. The influence of these biblical passages have come down to us in the West through the English Magna Carta, the establishment of the colony of Rhode Island on the platform of religious liberty, and the United States Bill of Rights.

The Protestant Reformation also contributed greatly toward personal freedom, legal rights, and political democracy. Although some Reformers were often authoritarian, even cruelly so, they helped prepare the way for a better world. Their concern for such themes as justification by faith, a growing recognition of the priesthood of all believers, the importance of individual conscience, and the need for personal interpretation of the Bible produced followers deeply conscious of their inherent worth, who would soon demand freedom under God in every area of life.

Further, the increased recognition of secular vocations and the larger role given the laity in the Protestant ministry and church government prepared future generations for the legal rights and responsibilities of democracy. One example is Thomas Helwys's defiant claim for religious liberty when he wrote his ruling monarch, King James I of England: "Heare O King. . . . The King is a mortall man, and not God therefore hath no power over ye immortall soules of his subjects, to make lawes and ordinances for them, and to set spirituall Lords over them."[15]

A Land that I Will Show You

The night before the Puritan-Pilgrims arrived on the shores of what would later be called New England, they drafted and signed the Mayflower Compact. This was the beginning of a new nation founded not on the divine rights of kings or military might, but on democratic principles granted and undergirded by God as the Creator of all. The

Christian inspiration and orientation of the document are unmistakable:

> We whose names are underwritten, having undertaken, for the glory of God, and advancement of the Christian faith, a Voyage to plant the first colony in the northern parts of Virginia, do, in the presence of God and one of another, covenant and combine ourselves together into a Civil Body Politic, for our better ordering and preservation, and furtherance of the ends aforesaid, and, by virtue hereof, to enact, constitute and frame such just and equal laws, ordinances, acts, constitutions, offices, from time to time, as shall be thought most meet and convenient for the general good of the Colony. . . .[16]

While it may appear that this new concept of society established on basic spiritual principles was far too late appearing in history, the tremendous distance between this political ideal and those in force at the time of Christ should not be overlooked.

Even though these early settlers did not always live up to their highest intentions, the spirit of freedom and equality continued to advance. When Roger Williams and the Baptists were not granted religious liberty in Massachusetts, Williams founded Rhode Island with the political guarantee that

> no person within the said colony, at any time hereafter, shall be any wise molested, punished, disquieted, or called in question, for any differences in opinion in matters of religion, who do not actually disturb the civil peace of our said colony; but that all and every person and persons may, from time to time, and at all times hereafter, freely and fully have and enjoy his and their own judgments and consciences in matters of religious concernments, throughout the tract of land hereafter mentioned; they behaving themselves peaceably and quietly.[17]

As individuals and members of nations and institutions, we still struggle to realize these ideals and need the grace to grant them to others. There should, however, be little doubt regarding the role of Christ in shaping and helping us reach these goals.

And the Truth Shall Make You Free

The New England Puritans not only professed a love for freedom and democracy but also sought to undergrid these concerns by establishing possibly the first truly public schools in history. Learning was no longer to be for the privileged few but the right and opportunity of everyone. It is, therefore, not surprising that the early American universities were all church sponsored and supported. Harvard was founded for the education of ministers just sixteen years after the Pilgrims landed on American soil. Then came William and Mary, Yale, Princeton, and King's College which became Columbia University. While these universities were basically Puritan in spirit, they owed much of their inspiration and heritage to those first great universities, the church schools of Paris, Oxford, Bologna, and Salerno.

The Pursuit of Excellence

Since the Christian revelation came after centuries of human development and learning and after the rise and fall of many civilizations, there is neither desire nor need to claim that Christianity inaugurated higher education. The rabbinical schools of the Old Testament, the Egyptian traditions of arts and crafts, Hippocrates's fraternity of medicine, Plato's Academy, and many other similar institutions contributed to education. However, the Christian tradition, with its emphasis upon the wisdom of God and the high priority given to His Word, has inspired and sustained the pursuit of truth and academic excellence in many fields. The Christian believes not only that Christ is the Creator of the world but also that He intended it to be understood, cultivated, and enjoyed.

The Desire to Read

The conviction that the Bible, and particularly the New Testament, provided instruction for abundant living and the indispensable truth needed for eternal salvation has motivated millions throughout the ages to learn to read. This has in turn opened new horizons in language, science, and the arts. One of the first great libraries in the world was founded in Alexandria, Egypt, in the third century AD by Clement and Origen as an outgrowth of their Christian instruction to new converts.

That the clergy was the most educated class of society from just after New Testament times until the Renaissance is commonly accepted. Yale historian Kenneth Scott Latourette ventured that

More than any other religion, or, indeed, than any other element in human experience, Christianity had made for the intellectual advance of man in reducing languages to writing, creating literatures, promoting education from primary grades through institutions of university level, and stimulating the human mind and spirit to fresh explorations into the unknown.[18]

One of the great ironies of history is that in recent times advanced learning, particularly in science, is believed by many to make the Christian faith obsolete.

The Books of Nature

Modern science owes its very existence to the Christian religion and its orderly, systematic theology. God, through Christ, created a world endowed with personal worth and one stable enough to be investigated. Of all the adventurers into the natural world, the Christian was best prepared to discover its designs and mysteries as though they had been personally autographed and guaranteed valuable by their author.

While the established church has sometimes retarded the progress of science and has been guilty of arrogant repression on some occasions, it has nonetheless provided the inspiration and insight for many important discoveries. The Christian recognition of the value of experiencing God personally rather than just speculating about Him became the foundation, through Roger Bacon, for the beginnings of modern science. Bacon's conviction that we should not just imagine things about God but should look into history and His Word where He has revealed Himself was the model for the experimental or inductive method of science. Just as Bacon had tried to be sensitive to the Bible as God's Book, so he sought to make his interpretations in science correspond to the "books of nature."[19]

Although many complex factors contributed to the origin and development of science, it is historical fact that science emerged in the West from a civilization that had been profoundly influenced by medieval Christian theology. Stanley L. Jaki explained that

> science suffered a stillbirth not only in Greece but in all great ancient cultures, in India, in China, in pre-Columbian America, in Egypt, and in Babylon. A careful reading of their philosophical, religious, and scientific documents, many of which are available in modern language translations, indicates a common factor of those stillbirths. The factor

was the belief in an eternal, cyclic recurrence of everything in a universe which was taken as the ultimate entity.[20]

The Christian, however, maintained that God was the Creator of nature. Every manifestation and episode in nature (whether directly caused by God or merely allowed in human freedom) could somehow be intelligently and systematically related to the stability and purposefulness of God.

The Splendor of Holiness

Christianity has also enriched the arts. From their Old Testament heritage, Christians understand that in the beginning the universe was without form and void until God called it into being with His creative Word. Then the world was formed in purposefulness, order, stability, symmetry, harmony, radiance, and *beauty.* We read in the creation story that after God made the world He "saw all that he had made, and it was very good" (Gen. 1:31). Among many other wonderful themes, God was surely saying, "This is beautiful!" Just as artists sign their paintings when they are pleased to acknowledge their work, so God, the first artist, commended the beauty of His world.

Christians are encouraged, "whatever you do, do it all for the glory of God" (1 Cor. 10:31). Wherever this message has been received, artists of all cultures and art forms have received inspiration, consciously or unconsciously, to recognize and reflect the beauty of the Lord and His creation through their art. Christian interpreters of art through the ages may, therefore, welcome every beautiful artistic creation and believe that these works are possible only because God has placed beauty so abundantly at the disposal of the artist.

Echoes of the Word

It is impossible to imagine literature without the simplifying, purifying influence of the New Testament narratives and discourses. Christ's crisp penetrating speech patterns and His unique employment of the parable as a literary form have enhanced language and literature throughout the world. When Dante wrote his *Divine Comedy,* it was as though the church was saying to the ancient writers like Homer and Virgil, "We will with gratitude accept your literary contributions, but now, allow us to revitalize your narratives with historical substance and enliven your imagination with the imagery of eternity."

John Wycliffe, the "morning star of the Reformation," gave England its very first Bible translated into English. More than any other single book, this volume standardized the grammar, vocabulary, and style of the English language. Many sought to burn the copies as they appeared, but the Word of God, especially in this language of the people, could not be restrained. Thirty years after Wycliffe's peaceful death in England, the Council of Constance ruled that his body be dug up, burned, and his ashes thrown into a tiny stream that runs past Lutterworth into the Avon River. A poet of that day voiced a hope that has long since come true:

> The Avon to the Severn runs,
>   The Severn to the sea;
> And Wyclif's dust shall spread abroad
>   Wide as the waters be.[21]

The truth of the Word of God was destined to be spread abroad and, along with it, the permeating Christian influence on language and literature.

New Wine in New Wineskins

Christian sculptors like Michelangelo and Bernini inherited the often cold, formal beauty of Greek statues and gave their marble forms a face, a personality with purpose for living and a worthy destiny. Rembrandt's portraits were not merely representations but character studies of the subjects' depth and worth. They revealed from a Christian perspective the individuality of people with sins, guilt and anxieties, shadows and scars—yet with the hope, promise, and, at times, the radiance of forgiveness and redemption.

The church was also responsible for enriching the chords and harmonies of music, perhaps because the simple, monotonous, limited scales of ancient music were not expansive enough to express God's abundant grace and Christian joy. The grand beauty of the Gothic cathedrals owe their majesty to the pious desires of the believers to express their faith with a building appropriate to the massive stability, intricate complexity, and radiant glory of God. And if we had nothing more than the beautifully illustrated biblical manuscripts of the medieval period, we could thank the church for ennobling landscape art. In yet another area, when John Bunyan wrote *The Pilgrim's Progress,* he gave the world not only a Christian devotional classic but also, many believe, its first novel.

A Cloud of Witnesses

It is not possible to discuss here many of the other contributions Christ and His church have made to history, but some others at least should be mentioned. The elimination of the gladiatorial combats in ancient Rome, the elevation of women, prison reform, the eradication of cannibalism, and the creation of protective structures for marriage and family life have all been areas where Christ's influence has been constructive.

The church has also been instrumental in banning foot-binding in the Orient, the burning of widows in India, and has spoken wise warnings against astrology, superstition, gambling, and drug abuse. It continues to strive for better relations among races, a wholesome balance between the recognition of material needs and spiritual welfare, and world peace beginning with individuals and extending through international relationships. Much remains to be done in most of these areas, but it would be staggering to imagine what the world today would be without the leavening influence of God's kingdom through the centuries.

Christians will not be surprised to read Latourette's generous assessment of the contributions of Christ to world history since he is a fellow believer. Christianity, he said, has been

> the largest single factor in combating, on a world-wide scale, such ancient foes of man as war, disease, famine, and the exploitation of one race by another. More than any other religion it had made for the dignity of human personality. This it had done by a power inherent within it of lifting lives from selfishness, spiritual mediocrity, and moral defeat and disintegration to unselfish achievement and contagious moral and spiritual power. It had also accomplished it by the high value which it set upon every human soul through the possibilities which it held out of endless growth and fellowship with the eternal God.[22]

However, it seems especially significant when an agnostic like T. H. Huxley is willing to acknowledge the beneficial impact of Christ:

Whoso calls to mind what I may venture to term the bright side of Christianity—that ideal of manhood, with its strength and patience, its justice and its pity for human frailty, its helpfulness to the extremity of self-sacrifice, its ethical purity and nobility, which apostles have pictured, in which armies of martyrs have placed their unshakable faith, and whence obscure men and women, like Catherine of Siena and John Knox, have derived courage to rebuke Popes and Kings—is not likely to underrate the importance of the Christian faith as a factor in human history.[23]

Any evidence for the Christian faith taken from the long stretches of history must admittedly be very selective. When the survey has been made, it is only another testimony with an invitation to believe. In history, as in nature, God has not left Himself without witnesses. Today, the spiritual alternatives between faith and unbelief are essentially the same as they were in the first-century world when the writer of Hebrews pleaded: "Therefore, since we are surrounded by such a great cloud of witnesses, . . . let us run with perseverance the race marked out for us. Let us fix our eyes on Jesus, the author and perfector of our faith" (Heb. 12:1-2).

An Unfinished Story

When we search history for signs that the Christian faith is true, we are continually reminded that history is not yet finished. We must then ask: Has the church made a good beginning? While many things remain to be accomplished, has it shown the capacity to meet the needs of all kinds of persons, cultures, and complex social situations? Has there appeared any opposition which seems capable of destroying it in the end? When true to its Lord and relying upon His spiritual resources, how does the church's future look? Just as individual Christians may be confident that "he who began a good work in you will carry it on to completion until the day of Christ Jesus" (Phil. 1:6), so we may believe that what God has begun in human history He will bring either to judgment, in keeping with the way He has made us free and responsible, or to glorious fulfillment.

At Caesarea Philippi, Christ promised that the gates of hell, Hades, or the realm of death would never overcome His church (Matt. 16:18). Baker James Cauthen, when president of the Southern Baptist Foreign Mission Board, was once criticized for allowing missionaries to remain on their fields during a time of war. He answered one of his critics respectfully but firmly: "My dear Christian friend, if I thought there was one possibility in a million of sending a missionary to hell, I would be in favor of sending that missionary." This kind of confidence must characterize believers as they look forward. We are to be on the offensive! Let us then be grateful for the church not just as it *has been* in history, but as it may *become* in the future.

Since the church is made up of individuals who, along with their civilizations and cultures, know periods of advance and decline, so we may expect its influence to ebb and flow. We have enough evidence now, however, not only to be confident of its survival but also to believe that it will continue to make enriching contributions as long as time shall last. Now it is no longer the church that is on trial—it is the human race.

Notes

1. D. T. Niles, "What Is the Church For?" *Princeton Seminary Bulletin* LVIII, No. 3 (June 1965), p. 9.

2. G. K. Chesterton, *The Everlasting Man* (London: Hodder and Stoughton, 1947), pp. 302-303.

3. "The First Epistle of Clement to the Corinthians", ch. 2, in *The Ante-Nicene Fathers* (New York: Scribners, 1903), 1:5.

4. "Epistle to Diognetus", chs. v and vi in *The Ante-Nicene Fathers*, 1:26, 27.

5. "Origen Against Celsus", Book III, ch. lix in *The Ante-Nicene Fathers* (Grand Rapids: Eerdmans, 1951), 4: 487-488.

6. J. Stevenson, ed., *Creeds, Councils and Controversies, Documents Illustrative of the History of the Church A.D. 337-461* (New York: Seabury, 1966), pp. 66-67.

7. S. L. Greenslade, *The Church and the Social Order* (London: SCM Press, 1948), p. 20.

8. Ibid, pp. 21-22.

9. W. E. H. Lecky, *History of European Morals* (London: Longmans, Green, 1911), 2:100.

10. W. E. H. Lecky, *Rationalism in Europe* (London: Longmans, Green, 1910), 1:326.

11. From *Songs from the Slums* by Toyohiko Kagawa. Copyright renewal © 1963 by Lois J. Erickson. Used by permission of the publisher, Abingdon Press.

12. W. Garden Blaikie, *The Personal Life of David Livingstone* (New York: Laymen's Missionary Movement, n.d.), pp. 480-481.

13. Harriet Beecher Stowe, *Uncle Tom's Cabin* (New York: Dodd, Mead & Co., 1952 [1853]), p. 333.

14. T. Plucknett, *A Concise History of the Common Law* quoted in Greenslade, pp. 53-54.

15. Thomas Helwys, *A Short Declaration of the Mistery of Iniquity* (London: Kingsgate, 1935, reproduced by Replika process from the copy presented by Helwys to King James) handwritten flyleaf preceding title page.

16. Frank S. Mead, *The March of Eleven Men* (Indianapolis: Bobbs-Merrill Co., 1931), pp. 187-188.

17. Roland H. Bainton, *The Church of Our Fathers* (London: SCM Press, 1947), p. 227.

18. Kenneth Scott Latourette, *Advance Through Storm* (New York: Harper & Row, 1945), p. 480-481.

19. T. F. Torrance, "Newton, Einstein and Scientific Theology," *Religious Studies* 8 (Sept. 1972), p. 233.

20. Stanley L. Jaki, "God and Creation: A Biblical-Scientific Reflection," *Theology Today* 30 (July 1973), p. 114.

21. Mead, p. 157.

22. Latourette, pp. 481.

23. A. R. Vidler, "Historical Objections," D. M. MacKinnon et al, *Objections to Christian Beliefs* (New York: Lippincott, 1964) p. 74.

10

Into All the World

Even though we are the ones who must believe in order to become Christians, faith is a divine personal gift which we receive when we are willing to accept both Christ's demands and His strength. It may happen dramatically, as when Saul of Tarsus asked the blinding risen Christ, "Who are you, Lord?"—and then obeyed Him (Acts 9:5); or possibly more gently, as when the first disciples simply "left their nets and followed him" (Mark 1:18).

But it can and should happen! It may take place at some mysterious but distinct point in time like that indescribable moment when the earth tilts on its axis and winter moves toward spring. Sometimes it is like that precious threshold you cross when you realize that a friend has really become someone you love—and you *know* this love is *forever.* We allow ourselves to be pulled out of the gravity of our own self-centered orbit and enter Christ's personal field of influence. This letting go of ourselves and coming under His lordship makes us Christians.

Breathing In and Out

Just as you could not hide your new love for a friend if you wanted to—and you don't—so love for Christ must be expressed. This need to declare our faith to the world is not optional for Christians nor merely some artificial requirement by the church. Christ commanded, "Whoever acknowledges me before men, I will also acknowledge him before my Father in heaven" (Matt. 10:32). Paul also underscored this need for a public profession of faith when he explained:

> If you confess with your mouth, "Jesus is Lord," and believe in your heart that God raised him from the dead, you will be saved. For it is

146

with your heart that you believe and are justified, and it is with your
mouth that you confess and are saved (Rom. 10:9-10).

This confession is an organic vital expression of our allegiance to
Christ made possible—indeed necessary—by His indwelling presence.
It is like being in life-giving air and *confessing* it by breathing out.

Augustine told of a conversion and profession of faith which,
though it happened 1,600 years ago, is as fresh as next Sunday morning's invitation in church to accept Christ and come forward to confess Him publicly. Victorinus, a teacher of rhetoric in ancient Rome,
had for years defended the pagan gods with a thundering eloquence.
One day he astonished his friend Simplicianus, a believer in Christ,
by declaring, "I am already a Christian." But his friend replied, "I will
not believe it, nor will I reckon you among Christians, unless I see you
in the Church." Victorinus laughed, "Is it walls, then, that make men
Christians?"

Later, suddenly and unexpectedly, Victorinus said to his friend,
"Let us go to the Church. I wish to become a Christian." He was given
instruction and the day was set for his public confession and baptism.
Augustine described the joyful celebration of love and acceptance:

> When he arose to make his profession, all who knew him uttered his
> name to one another with a murmur of congratulation. And who
> among them did not know him! A suppressed sound issued from the
> mouths of all those who rejoiced together, "Victorinus! Victorinus!"
> Suddenly, as they saw him, they gave voice to their joy, and just as
> suddenly they became silent in order to hear him. He pronounced the
> true faith with splendid confidence, and they all desired to clasp him
> to their hearts. By their love and joy they clasped him to themselves.
> Those were the hands by which they clasped him.[1]

Although the external circumstances may vary, this scene takes place
in spirit every time a believer enters the fellowship of Christ's church!

Room to Grow

One of the first things we learn when we become Christians is that
there is always room to grow. We are continually challenged to "reach
[for] unity in the faith and in the knowledge of the Son of God and
become mature, attaining to the whole measure of the fullness of
Christ" (Eph. 4:13). This involves discipline, but it is not an anxious

striving or beating of the wind. Rather, it is a dynamic goal adequately sustained by intimate personal fellowship with our Lord and His followers.

As we try to become more like Him, we need to understand and experience more fully what it means to love purely and unselfishly as He loves. We must learn increasingly to forgive our enemies, to penetrate the gloom and despair of our age, and to perceive without doubt or hesitation the ground of our hope.

At the beginning of our discipleship, we may be tempted to think too statically about the Christian life, as though it were like accumulating wealth, stamp collecting, or building a good library. We might even hope to become specialists in some spiritual areas and, with time, master our subject.

While there might be some value in these aims, the Christian life is overall more like climbing a mountain. Even though God's landscape of reality remains secure, He is always granting new visions and perspectives. Each vista on the climb provides unique challenges and greater possibilities for experiencing the joys of the abundant life. The thrilling thing is that Christ is our faithful guide and companion on the ascent. We learn more and more to follow in His steps up the slope. Though each danger provides its own testing in crisis, we gradually learn to trust Him as He leads and, on occasion, holds the ropes. He does not just know the way; He *is* the way (John 14:6). He is our Guide into truth and peace (John 16:13; Luke 1:79).

The Depths of Glory

Although the Christian life begins and continues in a spirit of surrender to Christ, we are also challenged and empowered to confront our world with both the story of Christ and with His desire that the kingdom, the rule, of God come upon earth (Matt. 6:10). We are not just invited to *believe* the resurrection of Christ and *receive* the assurance of our own resurrection, but we are commissioned to *oppose death* in all its forms! This includes the need for Christians to be involved on the spiritual front and in the secular, cultural trenches as well. These include such fields as the home, education, the arts, medicine, politics, and social action. We are, as Christ intended us to be, "in the world" (John 17:11). We, therefore, should be concerned to proclaim that Christ is Lord over all the world and to try to demonstrate His supremacy in all things (Col. 1:18).

As Christians we are never to live just for ourselves. We are to be the "salt of the earth" and "the light of the world" (Matt. 5:13-14). We should be His witnesses throughout the world, at home and abroad (Matt. 28:19; Acts 1:8). This means not only that we are to spread the gospel around the whole world geographically but also into every strata of society. We are to address the heights, middle, and depths of human need—those striving for excellence, those complacent in mediocrity, as well as those who have given up.

Springs of Gratitude

Peter sought to convince early church members that they should express their gratitude to God by witnessing for Him. He told them: "You are a chosen people, a royal priesthood, a holy nation, a people belonging to God, that you may declare the praises of him who called you out of darkness into his wonderful light" (1 Pet. 2:9).

This means, as Karl Barth reminded, that the fellowship of believers should never become preoccupied with its own well-being or functions:

> A Church that recognizes its commission will neither desire nor be able to petrify in any of its functions, to be the Church for its own sake. There is the "Christ-believing group;" but this group is *sent out:* "Go and preach the Gospel!" It does not say, "Go and celebrate services!" "Go and edify yourselves with the sermon!" "Go and celebrate the Sacraments!" "Go and present yourselves in a liturgy, which perhaps repeats the heavenly liturgy!" "Go and devise a theology which may gloriously unfold like the *Summa* of St. Thomas!" Of course, there is nothing to forbid all this; there may exist very good cause to do it all; but nothing, nothing at all for its own sake! In it all the one thing must prevail: "Proclaim the Gospel to every creature!"[2]

Barth tried to live by these convictions. I remember his turning down an invitation to visit with the graduate faculty and students at the University of Chicago on a Saturday morning during a visit to America. He had already made arrangements to preach at the state penitentiary of Illinois, just as he usually did on Saturdays to the prisoners at the Basel jail in Switzerland.

To See a Sermon

But we are not just to *speak* about the gospel and our faith. We are to *act* upon our convictions. One of the most significant events of modern times took place recently when scores of the top entertainers in popular music, superstars from many nations, gathered to record a song to benefit world hunger. In spite of vast differences in temperament, ethnic or political background, and life-style, they were united in their effort. The proceeds for their recording went, and continue to go, for those in desperate need of food. It was the first time anything like this had ever occurred on such a global scale with such immediate impact. Our world become more nearly one that day in January 1985 when they sang, "We Are the World."

While commending this noble concern and practical expression, a Christian has even better reasons and greater incentives to help people in need. We are not only one with the world in our common humanity, we are "the body of Christ." In a real and practical way we are His eyes, hands, and feet (1 Cor. 12:12-28).

No Turning Back

Very early in these pages I told you how as a small boy I became aware of my sins and need of a Savior. Some years have now passed since that day I became a Christian. You have every right to ask, "What has it been like, following Christ? Would you do it all over again?"

Since that day I have believed and doubted, stumbled and been forgiven, struggled forward and slipped back not quite so far—but never have I regretted becoming a Christian. Sometimes my witness has been received, but often it has been rejected. I have both caused and experienced hurt within my family and the church. On occasion I have known heartbreak within these circles which I still cannot believe. Now I wish that I were much more like those spiritual heroes of mine when I first began the journey—not to mention the distance remaining between me and my Lord. But always there has been more love, strength, and joy than hurt. His grace has been not only sufficient but also abundantly rich and rewarding. In times of death, sorrow, sickness, and many kinds of pain, Christ has been there. No turning back!

Once an early missionary to the British Isles, one of Colombo's followers, was interrupted in his sermon by the savage king of the Picts, who asked: "What would happen if I were to accept your message and become a Christian?" The missionary answered, "O King, you would stumble upon wonder after wonder, and every wonder true."

I stumbled upon a wonder behind John Wesley's magnificent church in old London when I discovered, to my surprise, the graceful marble spire that honors Wesley's life and marks his grave. On it are these simple moving words: "After languishing awhile in pain, he gave up the spirit and gained the victory over death." Now we can write on the monument of each new day: "Although languishing often in our own strength, we may surrender through the Spirit to the risen Lord and gain the victory over *life!*"

I began this book with *the* invitation for everyone to become a Christian and a picture of Christ standing outside a door, symbolizing the heart, knocking, and asking to enter. The question once raised by a small child who stood before this painting captures the burden of our concern: "Daddy, did He ever get in?"

Notes

1. Augustine, *Christian Classics,* "The Confessions," Bk.8, Ch. 2, ed. Douglas L. Anderson (Nashville: Broadman Press, 1979) pp. 164.

2. Karl Barth, *Dogmatics in Outline,* trans. G. T. Thomson (London: SCM, 1955), p. 147.

Scripture Index